HAZING:

rituals of bondage

Richard Lundeen

ALSO BY RICHARD LUNDEEN

Fraternity

Cocktails and Shots for Party's

Black Dagger

Boomers Reference Guide to American College Fraternities and Sororities

Duty Bound: A Guide to Bootcamp and to Basic Military Skills

HAZING: rituals of bondage

Published in the United States of America

Create Space, Charleston, SC.

Lundeen, Richard, 1963 –

1.   Hazing – Sociology – Popular Culture –non fiction
2.   Group Dynamics – Sociology – Popular Culture – non-fiction

ISBN 9781481061926

Printed in the United States of America

"I know it when I see it"
Justice Potter Stewart

CONTENTS

HAZING: rituals of bondage

The term hazing conjures up imagery of drunken students made to perform silly skits or some unlucky pledge being swatted with a paddle. But the reality is that hazing is a difficult subject to broach because of individual ideas of what hazing might be. To one person, a newbie forced to where a clowns outfit might be nothing more than fun and games, yet to another individual the forced wearing of a clown outfit is clearly hazing. Is tossing a person into a shower hazing? What about the infamous Navy traditions pertaining to WOG Day or Crossing the Equator ceremonies? Perhaps, then, the best language regarding hazing can come from Justice Potter Stewart when he stated, in 1964,with reference to obscenity, "I know it when I see it."

Those who haze often do so in a group circumstance. The evidence suggests that the unity of the group allows for hazing to take place. Without this, the group dynamic of unity, the fundamental elements which make hazing possible collapse. The research completed into the hazing phenomena suggest groups use hazing as a way of bonding not only with each other but as a way of social bonding with those being hazed regardless of the risks involved.

HAZING

Hazing" refers to any activity expected of someone joining a group (or to maintain full status in a group) that humiliates, degrades or risks emotional and/or physical harm, regardless of the person's willingness to participate. In years past, hazing practices were typically considered harmless pranks or comical antics associated with young men in college fraternities.

Today we know that hazing extends far beyond college fraternities and is experienced by boys/men and girls/women in school groups, university organizations, athletic teams, the military, and other social and professional organizations. Hazing is a complex social problem that is shaped by power dynamics operating in a group and/or organization and within a particular cultural context.

Hazing activities are generally considered to be: physically abusive, hazardous, and/or sexually violating. The specific behaviors or activities within these categories vary widely among participants, groups and settings. While alcohol use is common in many types of hazing, other examples of typical hazing practices include: personal servitude; sleep deprivation and restrictions on personal hygiene; yelling, swearing and insulting new members/rookies; being forced to wear embarrassing or humiliating attire in public; consumption of vile substances or smearing of such on one's skin; brandings;

8

physical beatings; binge drinking and drinking games; sexual simulation and sexual assault.

Some common definitions and examples of hazing are below:

In the Alfred/NCAA survey of college athletes, hazing was defined as:

"any activity expected of someone joining a group that humiliates, degrades, abuses or endangers, regardless of the person's willingness to participate. This does not include activities such as rookies carrying the balls, team parties with community games, or going out with your teammates, unless an atmosphere of humiliation, degradation, abuse or danger arises."

"Hazing is an activity that a high-status member orders other members to engage in or suggests that they engage in that in some way humbles a newcomer who lacks the power to resist, because he or she want to gain admission to a group. Hazing can be noncriminal, but it is nearly always against the rules of an institution, team, or Greek group. It can be criminal, which means that a state statute has been violated. This usually occurs when a pledging-related activity results in gross physical injury or death" (from Hank Nuwer's book Wrongs of Passage , 1999, p. xxv).

Hazing is defined by the FIPG (Fraternal Information Programming Group) as:

"Any action taken or situation created, intentionally, whether on or off fraternity premises, to produce mental or physical discomfort, embarrassment, harassment, or ridicule. Such activities may include but are not limited to the following: use of alcohol; paddling in any form; creation of excessive fatigue;

9

physical and psychological shocks; quests, treasure hunts, scavenger hunts, road trips or any other such activities carried on outside or inside of the confines of the chapter house; wearing of public apparel which is conspicuous and not normally in good taste; engaging in public stunts and buffoonery; morally degrading or humiliating games and activities; and any other activities which are not consistent with fraternal law, ritual or policy or the regulations and policies of the educational institution."

1. If you have to ask if it's hazing, it is.

2. If in doubt, call your advisor/coach/national office. If you won't pick up the phone, you have your answer. Don't B.S. yourself.

3. If you haze, you have low self-esteem.

4. If you allow hazing to occur, you are a 'hazing enabler.'

5. Failure to stop hazing will result in death.

The following are some examples of hazing divided into three categories: subtle, harassment, and violent. It is impossible to list all possible hazing behaviors because many are context-specific. While this is not an all-inclusive list, it provides some common examples of hazing traditions.

A. SUBTLE HAZING:

Behaviors that emphasize a power imbalance between new members/rookies and other members of the group or team. Termed "subtle hazing" because these types of hazing are often taken-for-granted or accepted as "harmless" or meaningless. Subtle hazing typically involves activities or attitudes that breach reasonable standards of mutual respect and place new members/rookies on the receiving end of ridicule, embarrassment, and/or humiliation tactics. New members/rookies often feel the need to endure subtle hazing to feel like part of the group or team. (Some types of subtle hazing may also be considered harassment hazing).

Some Examples:

Deception

Assigning demerits

Silence periods with implied threats for violation

Deprivation of privileges granted to other members

Requiring new members/rookies to perform duties not assigned to other members

Socially isolating new members/rookies

Line-ups and Drills/Tests on meaningless information

Name calling

Requiring new members/rookies to refer to other members with titles (e.g. "Mr.," "Miss") while they are identified with demeaning terms

Expecting certain items to always be in one's possession

B. HARASSMENT HAZING: Behaviors that cause emotional anguish or physical discomfort in order to feel like part of the group. Harassment hazing confuses, frustrates, and causes undue stress for new members/rookies. (Some types of harassment hazing can also be considered violent hazing).

Some Examples:

Verbal abuse

Threats or implied threats

Asking new members to wear embarrassing or humiliating attire

Stunt or skit nights with degrading, crude, or humiliating acts

Expecting new members/rookies to perform personal service to other members such as carrying books, errands, cooking, cleaning etc

Sleep deprivation

Sexual simulations

Expecting new members/rookies to be deprived of maintaining a normal schedule of bodily cleanliness.

Be expected to harass others

C. VIOLENT HAZING : Behaviors that have the potential to cause physical and/or emotional, or psychological harm.

12

Some Examples:

Forced or coerced alcohol or other drug consumption

Beating, paddling, or other forms of assault

Branding

Forced or coerced ingestion of vile substances or concoctions

Burning

Water intoxication

Expecting abuse or mistreatment of animals

Public nudity

Expecting illegal activity

Bondage

Abductions/kidnaps

Exposure to cold weather or extreme heat without appropriate protection

CASE LAW

During recent years, colleges and universities nationwide have witnessed a steady rise in hazing-related deaths and injuries, spawning a myriad of complex legal issues and considerations. Although hazing activities commonly occur in a variety of clubs and athletic teams, much of the existing case law pertains to Greek-letter organizations. Therefore, hazing within fraternities and sororities is often most noted. While once dismissed as a

13

few isolated cases caused by overzealous Greek members, hazing has developed into a disturbing trend, as more and more initially harmless pranks become potential lawsuits: "While fraternity misadventures comprise many a humorous tale, they may also leave multimillion dollar judgments, humiliation, disfigurement, crippling injury, and death in their wake" (Paine, 1994, p.191). But how much legal responsibility lies with the postsecondary institution-- or other institutions such as companies or the military establishment -- involved and what duty do they have to protect individuals from harm under these circumstances? This section of Hazing: rituals of bondage, will explore institutional liability regarding hazing. By examining key foundational cases, it will demonstrate how the university's legal stance has shifted from the in loco parentis doctrine to a "no duty" rationale in matters such as alcohol and hazing. Furthermore, it will consider the parallels and implications of state hazing statutes on institutional regulations, and offer suggestions for increasing compliance with hazing policies, subsequently minimizing the risk for potential institutional liability.

Within the context of fraternities and sororities, the term 'hazing' often invokes images of paddling, drinking games, and other "Animal House" antics. However, in reality it encompasses an extensive range of behaviors and activities, ranging from seemingly innocuous activities such as blindfolding and scavenger hunts, to more dangerous and extreme physical punishments, including sleep deprivation and excessive exercise. Currently, no singularly collective definition of hazing exists, and state laws differ with regard to what is considered criminal hazing. Nuwer (1999) defines hazing as "an activity that a high-status member orders other members to engage in or suggests that they engage in that in some way humbles a newcomer who lacks the power to resist, because he

14

or she wants to gain admission into a group" (p.xxv). Most traditionally-aged college students want to feel as if they belong to a group. Many regard hazing as an unpleasant but necessary task that must be endured in order to earn their membership: "For years...hazing has been viewed as a rite of passage – an initiation ceremony designed to determine one's worthiness as a prospective 'brother'" (Curry, 1989, p. 93). "Fitting in" is still quite salient at this stage of development, and courts have acknowledged the peer pressure element inherent in the pledging process (MacLachlan, 2000). Most students entering college and pledging Greek-letter organizations have reached the legal age of adulthood, yet their lack of emotional maturity may make them more susceptible to hazing or other potentially harmful activities. Therefore, to what extent should the college or university act as guardian or is it absolved of this duty altogether? In order to adequately address this question, it is essential to examine the evolution of institutional liability, particularly within the realm of the in loco parentis doctrine.

The Rise and Fall of the In Loco Parentis Doctrine:

Historically, colleges and universities were looked upon as "parental supervisors" to the students they enrolled: "Universities could control every facet of a student's life...the courts did not question the authority of colleges over their students" (MacLachlan, p.514). This line of reasoning - the basis of the in loco parentis doctrine - survived until the turbulent 1960s-1970s era, when societal attitudes and the relationships between students and colleges began changing. The demise of in loco parentis was partly due to the student rights litigation of the 1960s (MacLachlan, 2000), yet a procession of cases beginning with Bradshaw v. Rawlings (1975) unofficially put an end to the doctrine.

15

Bradshaw v. Rawlings and the Origin of the "No Duty" Rule:

In Bradshaw v. Rawlings (1975), two Delaware Valley College students attended a sophomore class picnic sponsored by the school. There was alcohol served and Rawlings became intoxicated. On the way back to campus, Bradshaw was a passenger in Rawling's vehicle. Rawling subsequently lost control of the car, struck a parked vehicle, rendering Bradshaw a quadriplegic. Bradshaw later sued the college - among others - claiming that it had breached its duty to protect him from unreasonable risk of harm. The fact that the students were "under age" was not enough to convince the court that they were entitled to supervision by the college. On appeal, the Third Circuit reversed the district court's judgment which had stated that the college should be held liable. The Third Circuit directed that a judgment in favor of the college be granted. Perhaps the Bradshaw decision is better put into context when one considers that it "was rendered at the same time that eighteen-year old college students were accepted as adult members of society" (MacLachlan, p. 516). The Third Circuit determined that since the students were no longer minors, there was no special relationship existing between the institution and the students that would constitute a duty on the part of the institution to control the conduct of a third party and to prevent him from harming another (Bradshaw v. Rawlings, 1975, as cited in Maclachlan, 2000).

The "No Duty" Trend Continues – Rabel v. Illinois Wesleyan University:

For several years, colleges and universities successfully utilized the Bradshaw decision as the precedent to escape liability for injuries to students during hazing-related rituals and activities (MacLachlan, 2000). Rabel v. Illinois Wesleyan University is

16

another example of this "no duty" movement. In this case, a female student (Rabel) suffered a basilar skull fracture and concussion after being forcibly grabbed, picked up, and accidentally dropped on the ground by a member of Phi Gamma Delta fraternity. Ms. Rabel filed a complaint against the university, alleging liability based on a landlord-tenant relationship. The university filed a motion for summary judgment, which was later granted by the trial court. Ms. Rabel appealed the dismissal, claiming that the "policies, regulations, and handbook created a special relationship with its students and a corresponding duty to protect its students against the alleged misconduct of a fellow student." (Rabel v. Illinois Wesleyan University, as cited in MacLachlan, 2000). The Appellate Court stated:

It would be unrealistic to impose upon a university the additional role of custodian over its adult students and to charge it with the responsibility for assuring their safety and the safety of others. Imposing such a duty of protection would place the university in the position of an insurer of the safety of its students.

(Rabel, as cited in MacLachlan, 2000).

Both of these rulings - combined with similar judgments in cases such as University of Denver v. Whitlock (1987) and Beach v. University of Utah (1986) - illustrate that institutions were unlikely to be held legally accountable for the actions and injuries of their students. The Bradshaw decision clearly established a "no-duty" model, in which courts concluded that "a custodial, supervisory relationship between a university and its students was inconsistent with modern educational objectives" (MacLachlan, p. 521). However, ensuing case law

17

would establish that – in certain circumstances – there is an assumed duty on the part of the institution.

Furek v. University of Delaware and the "No Duty" Exception:

After Bradshaw and its progeny of cases, attempts by plaintiffs to hold an institution liable for injuries sustained during hazing activities were mostly met with failure. However, the Furek (1991) decision demonstrated that courts were willing to impose liability on the university in "certain factual situations" (MacLachlan, p. 522). Although not entirely a revival of the in loco parentis doctrine, Furek signaled the demise of the absoluteness of the "no duty" movement.

In Furek v. University of Delaware, the plaintiff, a fraternity pledge, suffered first- and second-degree burns after a fraternity member poured oven cleaner over his head and back as part of Hell night high jinks. Attendance at the secret Hell night ceremony was mandatory for pledges in order to be accepted into the Sigma Phi Epsilon fraternity. The events took place in the chapter house, which was located on premises leased from the University of Delaware by the organization's alumni corporation. In addition, the university had an established policy prohibiting hazing. Ultimately, the Delaware Supreme Court found a duty on behalf of the university to protect its students from the hazards of hazing. "The adoption of a policy against hazing convinced the court that the university thereby exposed itself to liability for hazing-related injuries" (Furek v. University of Delaware, as cited in Paine, 1994). The court determined that the university's "pervasive" regulation of hazing amounted to an undertaking to protect its students from the dangers of hazing as well as a "correlative obligation to exercise appropriate restraint over [fraternity] members' conduct" (Kaplin and Lee, p. 421). Although the

18

university did not control the day-to-day activities of the chapter, it had an obligation to promote general campus safety and security.

Although most of the case law indicates that the Bradshaw line of reasoning is still a frequent and justifiable defense, the Furek decision is a landmark example of how the "no duty" principle is not applicable in every situation, particularly when hazing-related injuries are involved.

The contradictory elements of the in loco parentis and "no duty" arguments contribute profusely to the paradoxical relationship between universities and their students. On one hand, students want to be regarded as capable adults, trusted to make their own decisions. They participate in hazing activities, many of which go unreported. However, when someone is injured or harmed, they suddenly contend that the institution owed them a duty of protection: "The irony lies in the student plaintiff's assertion that he was not an adult capable of appreciating or avoiding the danger encountered" (Paine, p. 192). Perhaps Paine (1994) raises a valid question: "Why is a university liable for the violation of its anti-hazing policy when hazing generally occurs behind closed doors and beyond the view of the university?" (p.202).

What Does the Case Law Say About Hazing & Institutional Liability?

There is little debate that a duty must be found on the part of the institution in order for it to be held liable for death or injuries sustained from hazing. However, it becomes a muddier issue when attempting to prove that a duty existed. Furthermore, even if a duty is found, an institution still may not be found negligent unless the plaintiff is able to prove that "the institution's breach of duty was the proximate cause of the injury" (Kaplin and Lee, p. 97). Research of hazing case law indicates that when a duty has been found, the courts have generally concluded that although the institution may have a responsibility to regulate the conduct of the organization, it is not required to monitor the behavior of individual students. In addition, being enrolled as a student at the institution does not necessarily constitute a "special relationship." University of Denver v. Whitlock (1987) is an example of this reasoning. "The university did not have a special relationship based merely on the fact that Whitlock was a student" (Kaplin and Lee, p. 94).

Foreseeability is the determining factor in whether duty applies (MacLachlan, 2000). This is often evident when the institution has previously attempted to prohibit or control hazing activities (i.e., establishing anti-hazing policies, being aware of prior hazing incidents, etc.). Furek v. University of Delaware, discussed above, illustrates the importance of foreseeability. Knoll v. Board of Regents of the University of Nebraska (1999) is a further example. In this case, the plaintiff (Knoll, a fraternity pledge) was forcibly taken by active members from his residence hall to the fraternity house. The members forced him to a third floor bathroom and handcuffed him to a toilet. He was later able to break away from the toilet, and attempted to climb down an outside drainpipe, from which he fell and sustained serious injury. Knoll sued the university – among others – for negligence in protecting him from this danger. The university, in fact, had a policy prohibiting "pledge sneaks" unless they were registered in advance, and it had some awareness of various kinds of recent criminal behaviors in other fraternities on campus (particularly within this fraternity), including some instances of restraining individuals and forcing them to consume alcohol. Therefore, the Appellate Court ultimately reversed the District Court's earlier decision, concluding that:

The University could have foreseen various forms of student hazing on its property, even though [the fraternity] failed to disclose the pledge sneak event, including typical fraternity abductions and the consequences that could reasonably be expected to result from such activities

(Knoll v. Board of Regents, 1999).

Kaplin and Lee (1997) conclude that the presence of duty is a matter of state common law. Indeed, understanding states' hazing statutes and their pertinence to institutional liability adds another piece to the legal puzzle that is hazing.

State Hazing Statutes – Similarities & Differences:

The expanding body of case law pertaining to hazing points to the inescapable conclusion that these activities show little sign of diminishing. This inevitability has prompted an onslaught of legislative efforts to regulate hazing behaviors: "The states' rush to adopt anti-hazing legislation reflects the shift in society's view of hazing" (Curry, p. 116). Currently, 43 states have enacted statutes outlawing hazing or hazing-related actions, with Alaska, Hawaii, Montana, Michigan, New Mexico, South Dakota, and Wyoming being the exceptions. The similarities between states outweigh the differences with regard to what constitutes hazing. The definition of hazing varies only slightly, with some states offering broader definitions and others specifically designating hazing as an "initiation process." When examining the state laws collectively, common themes emerge. For example, the research indicates that in many states, "without bodily harm, there is no hazing" (Nuwer, p. 168). Most states define hazing as any activity endangering the physical health of the student.

However, some states – including Alabama, Ohio, Oklahoma, and Rhode Island - recognize the mental as well as the physical aspects of hazing. In most states, hazing is considered a misdemeanor, with fines ranging from $100 to $5000 (Manley, et al., 2000). In Illinois, Idaho, Missouri, Texas, Virginia, and Wisconsin, hazing resulting in death or "great bodily harm" is categorized as a felony. Perhaps one of the more progressive states in the area of hazing law, Florida has enacted three separate statutes governing state universities, community colleges, and public and private universities (Manley, et al., 2000). The New Hampshire law is also particularly aggressive, stating that institutions may also be charged with a misdemeanor for "knowingly condoning hazing or negligently failing to take adequate measures to prevent student hazing"

Many states contain stipulations outlining stiff punishment for those aiding or assisting in hazing activities. It is also evident that lawmakers acknowledge the significance of the peer pressure and coercion components of hazing: "In the vast majority of states, consent by the pledge or new member is not a defense to hazing"

Some states place the burden of enacting and enforcing anti-hazing regulations on the college or university. For example, Delaware, Pennsylvania, and Tennessee require all institutions to adopt a written anti-hazing policy. Florida and Kentucky take this a step further by requiring all institutions to also establish penalties for those violating anti-hazing rules. Furthermore, most of the state laws mandate the suspension or expulsion of students found guilty of hazing behavior. Indiana offers immunity for the "good faith reporting of hazing or participation in a judicial proceeding"

The most apparent similarities in these state laws involve their definitions of hazing as a physical crime and the classification of hazing as a misdemeanor. Some of the language in the statutes is rather vague and ambiguous, thereby granting an easier defense for the accused. For example, Louisiana and Kansas's statutes prohibit behavior that could "reasonably be expected to result in great bodily harm" (Manley, et al., 2000). The wording in these states' laws makes it probable that hazing would be more challenging to concretely prove. Many students who are being charged with hazing crimes are increasingly relying on this defense. Nonetheless, courts are overwhelmingly apt to find that the phrasing in the laws is sufficiently clear and understandable, as demonstrated by State v. Allen (1995). Allen was charged with five counts of hazing after he was accused of physically abusing five Kappa Alpha Psi pledges. One of those pledges died as a result of the beatings that were administered by Allen. Allen was convicted on all five counts. He later appealed his conviction to the Missouri Supreme Court arguing that "the [Missouri] hazing statutes were vague and overbroad" (Allen, 1995, as cited in MacLachlan, 2000). The Supreme Court subsequently resolved that the statute "clearly delineates its reach in words of common understanding. The statute is, therefore, not vague" (Allen, 1995, as cited in MacLachlan, 2000).

Undoubtedly, legislation has come a long way during the last decade to combat hazing behavior. However, after examining the laws, it is evident that more progress must be made in the way of providing more specific and inclusive definitions of hazing, as well as imposing heavier punishments for hazing offenses. Nuwer (1999) asserts that states must be more consistent with their hazing laws, and present a more united front: "Unless that happens, the same activity that designates a

23

hazer in one state as a criminal...is going to result in no criminal liability whatsoever in another state" (p.175).

Now more than ever, colleges and universities are faced with the complex dilemma of how to monitor the conduct and behavior of their Greek organizations: "Two diametrically opposed strategies present themselves to administrators: (1) exercising very strict control over fraternities; or (2) exercising no control whatsoever" (Curry, p. 111). As mentioned above, many state laws now place a heavy burden upon the institution, particularly with regard to adopting explicit anti-hazing policies. Yet at what point do state laws and institutional policies intersect? Case law precedent designates that the more tightly an institution attempts to control its Greek organizations, the more legal responsibility it ultimately assumes. Thus, colleges and universities are faced with choosing between two extremes: "strict policing or disassociation" (Curry, p. 111). In order to escape potential liability, many institutions are opting for "recognition statements" for Greek organizations (similar to those used to recognize other student organizations) in place of extensive regulation. However, as Kaplin and Lee note, "[Although] this minimal approach may defeat a claim that the institution has an assumed duty...it may limit the institution's authority to regulate the activities of the organization" (p. 421).

Recognition by an institution is often significant to the local success of national Greek organizations. Furthermore, the conditions under which the college awards recognition is especially important "because they may determine, or enhance, the college's power to regulate the conduct of the organization or its members" (Kaplin and Lee, p. 420). This has particular relevance when applied to hazing, as an increasing number of institutions are banning fraternities altogether (i.e.,

Colby College), while others (i.e., Middlebury, Bowdoin, and Trinity Colleges) have reasoned that hazing and binge-drinking would be halted by requiring fraternities and sororities to admit members of both sexes into their memberships (Kaplin and Lee, 1997).

The question of whether an institution is public or private adds another element to consider, particularly when the university seeks to outlaw fraternities and sororities. For example, public institutions face constitutional barriers, "including the First Amendment's guarantee of the right to associate" (Kaplin and Lee, p. 421). Issues regarding due process may also come into play when a private institution attempts to discontinue a Greek organization. A case in point is Mu Chapter of Delta Kappa Epsilon v. Colgate University (1992). The dean of Colgate University, a private university, suspended the chapter for one year and placed it on probation for another year after it was revealed that the members had engaged in hazing activities that violated the school's policy (Rutledge, 1998). This specified that the fraternity could not pledge any new member or sponsor or co-sponsor any social event for two years (Mu Chapter, 1992, as cited in Rutledge, 1998). The alumni corporation of the chapter appealed to the New York Supreme Court on the grounds that it should receive the full due process queue. In addition, they sought to have the incident removed from university records. The court disagreed, ruling that private universities were less restricted to constitutional parameters than their state-supported counterparts: "The university is not bound, unlike public universities, by the Fourteenth Amendment, and need only 'substantially comply' with its published guidelines...regarding procedures in a disciplinary proceeding" (Mu Chapter, 1992, as cited in Rutledge, 1998).

Despite the criminalizing of hazing in a vast majority of states, university officials at public as well as private institutions still grapple with hazing regulation on their respective campuses. State laws impose civil punishment on the individual perpetrators of hazing, yet overall, do little to address possible consequences for the chapter as a whole. This appears to be the crux of the regulation dichotomy for institutions, and it is a legal catch-22: Too much regulation of Greek organizations may constitute an implied duty; yet not enough will invoke institutional liability according to state law. The fact that many state laws require institutions to adopt anti-hazing policies is indicative that the trend is gradually moving toward a more comprehensive approach to hazing liability. State laws appear to be sending the message that not only should the individual students involved in hazing be punished, their institutions must also assume at least partial responsibility for not adequately monitoring and regulating hazing more closely. Therefore, with regard to the regulation/no regulation debate, Curry (1989) asserts that university administrators must strike a delicate balance between stringent regulation and passive detachment.

Minimizing Liability Risk:

College and university administrators are gradually realizing that it is not enough to merely establish anti-hazing policies and procedures. Consistently enforcing these regulations via risk education is the logical next step toward diminishing the likelihood of potential hazing occurrences, or – at the very least – demonstrating that the institution is committed to addressing the severity of hazing: "A good risk management program will decrease lawsuits which will inevitably threaten an institution's reputation and financial stability" (Davis, 2002). According to Davis (2002), an essential component of an effective risk management program is the question of risk control. With regard to managing hazing risk, institutions must address three essential components:

1) Supervision when there is knowledge of or involvement in activities known to be hazardous;

2) Procedures in place to deal with emergency situations...;

3) Resources...and other necessary supplies required to deal with potentially risky activities" (Davis, 2002). This also involves making senior officials available for deposition and trial who can testify about the purpose of risk management procedures (Fierberg, 2002).

Rutledge (1998) contends that cooperation in enforcement among postsecondary institutions and Greek organizations is a paramount strategy for reducing the risk of legal battles involving hazing. Yet unfortunately, colleges and Greek organizations often stand as adversaries when each are named as defendants in hazing lawsuits, as they are both attempting to minimize their own liability. Furthermore, when an institution imposes sanctions on fraternity or sorority members engaging in minor hazing incidents, these same individuals may receive little or no reprehension from their chapter. This punitive incongruity sends a clear and grossly misguided message to students: 'Hazing is acceptable as long as we aren't caught.' Universities and Greek organizations are capable of shifting these erroneous attitudes if they took a more unified stance toward hazing: "Fines, suspensions, and withdrawal of privileges are among the actions both colleges and universities and Greek organizations may take to penalize wrongdoing students and fraternity members" (Rutledge, 1998). Undoubtedly, the implementation of anti-hazing policies should define which hazing behaviors constitute which punishments and these should be enforced with consistency and regularity.

Summary and Conclusion:

Hazing litigation involving colleges and universities has increased significantly over the last few decades. Research for this book has demonstrated that while landmark cases such as Bradshaw v. Rawlings provide ample precedent for the "no duty" defense, recent hazing case law predicts that the trend toward institutional liability with regard to hazing will continue.

The majority of states have enacted fairly uniform laws prohibiting hazing, yet state law in this area is still in its nascent stages, as legislators struggle with arriving at clear, comprehensive definitions of hazing. In addition, more states are now recognizing the legal role of institutions by requiring them to establish anti-hazing policies that are more integrative and encompassing in nature.

Institutional regulation of hazing is a complex and twofold issue. Undeniably, some control is expected as well as necessary, yet the institution's extent of involvement may open the door to subsequent liability. Furthermore, public and private institutions face varying obstacles when attempting to regulate the behavior of their student organizations.

Effectively reducing hazing incidents and potential institutional liability involves a consistent combination of risk management programs and proactive strategies. Research indicates that risk management programs are more successful when Greek organizations and university administrators address hazing collectively rather than separately.

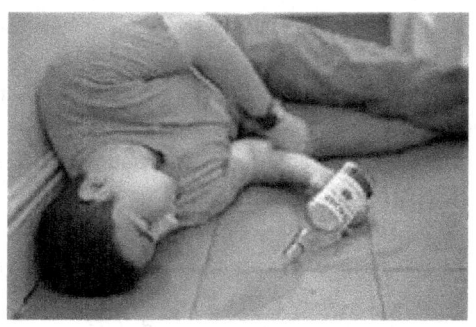

This part of the research sought to examine hazing liability from an institutional perspective. Yet this only begins to address the myriad of layers comprising hazing litigation. Indeed, case law has illustrated that the issue is not as black-and-white as one might initially perceive. The question of duty comes into focus in most hazing cases involving colleges and universities. However, the extent of that duty appears to be the determining factor regarding institutional liability. Above all, until hazing liability encompasses a multi-dimensional scope involving institutions, local and national Greek organizations, and individual chapter members, college students will continue to incur serious injury or death as a result of these senseless rituals.

. . .

Anti-hazing Statutes (2002). Retrieved from http://www.thegreekshop.com/hazing.html

Curry, S.J. (1989). Hazing and the "rush" toward reform: Responses from universities,

fraternities, state legislatures, and the courts. Journal of College and University

Law, 16(1), 93-117.

Davis, D.P. (2002). Tort law in higher education. Retrieved October 2, 2002 from

Fierberg, D.E. (2002). Representing victims of hazing and other group violence on campus.

Hennessy, N.J., & Huson, L.M. (1998). Legal issues and Greek letter organizations.

New Directions for Student Services, 81, 61-77.

Kaplin, W.A., & Lee, B.A. (1997). A legal guide for student affairs professionals.

San Francisco: Jossey-Bass.

Knoll v. Board of Regents (1999). Retrieved October 28, 2002 from

MacLachlan, J. (2000). Dangerous traditions: Hazing rituals on campus and university

liability, Journal of College and University Law, 26(3), 511-548.

Manley, Burke, Lipton, & Cook (2000). Hazing: Know the consequences of your

actions. The FRMT Risk Management Newsletter, 7, 1-3.

Nuwer, H. (1999). Wrongs of passage: Fraternities, sororities, and binge drinking.

Bloomington, IN: Indiana University Press.

Paine, E.A. (1994). Recent trends in fraternity-related liability. Journal of Law and

Education, 23(2), 191-210.

Rutledge, G.E. (1998). Hell night hath no fury like a pledge scorned...and injured:

Hazing litigation in U.S. colleges and universities. Journal of College and University Law, 25(2), 361-397.

State Anti-hazing Laws (2002). Retrieved September 21, 2002 from

30

HIGH SCHOOL HAZING

CASE HISTORY 1 [1]
La Puenta, California

As a child, the boy would pretend to be his favorite soccer pro, sliding across the ground and narrating into an imaginary microphone, "Oh, what a save by Oswaldo Sanchez!" But his mother thought the game was too rough. So he could only play pickup.

When he entered La Puente High, his mother decided to let him play. What authorities have said happened next was staggering, and led to the arrest of four students in September.

According to Los Angeles County sheriff's officials, older soccer players sodomized younger ones — and attempted to sodomize the youth, who requested anonymity. The youth said they used a sharpened pole and called the hazing ritual "giving the palo."

Three students currently face various charges of sexual assault and battery in the hazing case. This week in court, they denied the accusations. Charges were rejected against the fourth player for insufficient evidence.

I was dumbfounded that such an atavistic rite allegedly could have taken place on a modern high school campus. So I met with the youth and his mother to find out more.

We sat in his aunt's living room in a modest ranch-style home in La Puente, around the corner from the cul-de-sac where he and his cousins learned to kick the ball around.

The 15-year-old is slight, with dark wavy hair and an enviably clear complexion for a kid his age. He spoke mostly in a monotone, only showing emotion when his mother described how he had changed since the alleged assault: fighting at school, getting angry. It seemed he couldn't stand to cause his mother more suffering. She'd cried enough.

When he first heard the older soccer players talk about giving the palo, the youth told me, he thought it was just a story made up to scare the younger kids. Even after he saw another player limp — red-faced and furious — out of a storage room the varsity players used as their locker room, he wasn't sure the hazing was real.

But in a civil claim filed against the school district, the youth describes being ordered one day last spring to put equipment away in the varsity changing room. The space, just four steps away from his coach's desk, was rumored to be where the hazing happened, he told me.

The claim details his fear, and how he asked the coach, Bahram Alavi, if he could clean his office instead. But a player came out of the locker room and said he needed the younger boy in the back; Alavi winked at the older player as he was led away, according to the youth and the claim.

The coach, who has not been charged in the criminal case, could not be reached for comment.

"Right there, I thought what everybody had been saying was true," the youth said during our conversation. Once in the room, he alleged being jumped from behind and beaten. The claim describes players trying to stick the palo inside him, and him fighting them off. The bell rang, he told me, and his alleged attackers let him go.

The youth told me that when he staggered out, "All I heard was the coach laughing."

Hacienda La Puente Unified School District Supt. Barbara Nakaoka, in a written notice to parents, said that observers had likened the scandal to the Penn State sexual abuse case, but she argued that the comparison was unfair.

She's got a point. Unlike Penn State, where officials have been charged with failing to take action for years after learning about abuse allegations against coach Jerry Sandusky, the district notified authorities as soon as the alleged hazing was reported. And I take Nakaoka at her word that she personally was appalled.

"I thought it was the most horrible thing I ever heard of," Nakaoka said in an interview.

But if ritual hazing has in fact been occurring in the La Puente soccer program for years, it raises so many questions:

Is it something to do with sports culture? (Similar allegations have been brought outside of the team structure: In Fontana, a teacher was charged with sex abuse after a student allegedly was sodomized last summer during a masonry class. That case is ongoing.)

Are certain boys targeted because they are perceived as powerless?

One thing is certain: Abuse flourishes in silence.

When the palo rite was first reported, the youth said, his teammates called a meeting to get everyone to keep their mouths shut. He went.

Feeling pained or embarrassed, the youth at first denied he'd been attacked. Later, he told administrators the story he told me, he said, because "I didn't want what happened to me to happen to anyone else."

In our conversation, he said they acted like he was "stupid" and told him he had no evidence. His mother was mostly quiet through the interview, but became indignant talking about school officials. She said the principal had told her that since her son hadn't been penetrated, he was "all right, everything's fine."

The principal, Ava Smalley, declined to comment and referred all questions about the incident to the superintendent.

I'm not sure what happened here. But I would have liked to hear from the young accuser that officials had asked how they could help him and his family.

The youth is at another school now. Some of the kids there have heard the story and make fun of him, he said, but the school lets him take a time-out to compose himself. He's getting counseling.

His grades have fallen too low to play soccer, but if he can pull them up, he'll be the varsity goalkeeper, he said.

. . .

1 Gale Holland, "Three La Puente students face various charges including sexual assault. An accuser's mother is angry at the school's response." *Los Angeles Times*. 23 November 2012.

Reitz Memorial High School, in Evansville, Ind., bills itself as "providing an exceptional educational opportunity," while offering "a Christian community where young people are valued and cherished." The 87-year-old school has a rich sporting tradition—Tigers teams have won numerous state titles in football, baseball, girls tennis, and boys soccer, and even have a pair of national championships. But one thing's relatively new to Memorial: it wasn't until 1967 that the school first allowed female cheerleaders.

Cheer is big business at Memorial now. Just after the beginning of summer vacation, the entire 30-member Memorial team attended a four-day, "elite" level cheer camp held by the Universal Cheerleaders Association at the University of Tennessee. It's an annual tradition for Memorial; the team has been going to Knoxville every summer for more than a decade. It's fun, it's instructive, it's good for bonding.

This time though, "something" happened.

Last week, the school's president cryptically acknowledged an incident at the cheer camp, steadfastly refusing to go into detail.

"Recently the administration of Reitz Memorial High School became aware of an incident involving the school's cheerleading squad," Memorial President Brother Lawrence Murphy said in a statement released Tuesday. "The school has concluded an extensive investigation and will not comment publicly on the investigation or any action taken by the high school on the basis that all personnel and student disciplinary matters are private and confidential."

The local paper had a brief mention of the statement, and left it at that. But a Catholic school community has its own ecosystem, and it wasn't long before rumors began making the rounds. The final straw: a two-page anonymous letter, written by the mother of one of the girls who attended cheer camp, purporting to reveal the details on what happened in Knoxville. The letter was sent to media outlets and dropped in random mailboxes around Evansville, and one resident forwarded it to us.

Some highlights, followed by the full letter:

"The juniors went into the bathroom and all pooped in the same toilet, intentionally not flushing. The sophomores were then locked in the bathroom and told that if they flushed they would be in trouble. After locking them in a stall with a poop-filled toilet, they made the sophomore girls strip and give lap dances on the junior girls who had also taken clothes off. Throughout these lap dances, the juniors treated it as a contest that they judged ... The girls were insulted the entire time and called fat and ugly. They made fun of one girl's boyfriend and made her give a lap dance four times because she was not doing it correctly. The abuse went on for three hours. According to my daughter, many of the sophomores were crying, one girl even peed herself because she was so scared."

"The abuse was reported to the school and during the investigation the juniors admitted to school officials everything that they had done. The juniors said that they did not want to, however the coaches Jill Mitchell and Kim Schmidt told them that this was a tradition that had been going on for 15 years and that it was team bonding and that it would bring them closer together."

"Now, with school back in session the sophomores have been forced to face their abusers daily and endure harassment from the junior and senior cheerleaders. The sophomores have been threatened by the upperclassmen cheerleaders on Tweeter [sic], and are being bullied during school for coming forward and reporting the abuse from camp."

Mitchell and Schmidt both denied the claims made against them—though they quickly resigned. Mitchell gave a statement to 14 News, in which she said that "if hazing happened during my watch, I would not have condoned it, and if I had been advised of the situation that took place, I would have immediately reported it to the athletic director. It is unfortunate and disappointing to me that the person who wrote the letter didn't sign it."

14 News also spoke to a student who was at the camp, who confirmed many of the claims in the letter, including the lap dances, the cheerleader wetting herself with fear, and the coaches' justification when told about the hazing.

"The level of nudity varied by girl to girl, down to taking off their shirts, to their sports bras, underwear. Same with the

37

junior girl, who the lap dances were given on, was declothed down to her bra and spankies and there may have been some fondling involved."

The person says when they went to tell the now former head coaches, Jill Mitchell and Kim Schmidt. After the incident happened, they were told it was a Memorial High School tradition.

"This was a bonding experience that would keep them closer together."

The school still refuses to comment on the allegations in the letter or the results of its investigation. It confirms only that some students have been disciplined and three coaches asked to resign.

"Reitz Memorial High School has never and will never tolerate any behavior from our students that is inappropriate, intimidating, or which makes others feel uncomfortable or unsafe in any way. We take the welfare and safety of all of our students extremely seriously, and we are firmly committed to providing a safe, healthy, Christian environment for our students, both in and out of the classroom."

. . .

2 Barry Petchesky. "Catholic School Cheerleader Hazing Involved Poopy Lap Dances, Claims This Anonymous Letter Placed In Mailboxes Across Town". *Deadspin.com.* 2012.

When members of a high-school football team on Long Island were accused of sexual attacks, the community was appalled . . . some by the crimes, others by the cancellation of the season. Now the boys may face adult charges, the victims are being ostracized, and the locals are divided.

On the Offensive: Football practice at W.C. Mepham High School on September 10, a week before the season was called off.

(Photo: Joel Cairo of Newsday)

The star lineman towers over most of the other pallbearers. That blond buzz cut, the baby face, the meager beginnings of a goatee—he's only 16, too young to be burying his father. His broad shoulders are slumped and trembling as he walks the coffin down the aisle of Saint Barnabas Church in Bellmore, Long Island.

Bells toll. The parishioners sing "Make Me a Channel of Your Peace." And then the young lineman, who charged onto the varsity squad his sophomore year at W.C. Mepham High

School—Home of the Pirates—is in tears. Four days ago, his father died in his sleep. He was 40 years old. The priest declares that the father "had nothing but life ahead of him. What went wrong? We don't always understand, and we don't always see." He attempts a little levity—"I know he shared his hopes for the Yankees with the Lord"—before straining for profundity: "The great artist has finished his portrait." He urges the mourners to say a prayer for the family.

Everyone in the pews has heard how the father had been devastated by the criminal charges his son was facing. Aggravated assault. False imprisonment. Terroristic threats. Criminal coercion. Involuntary deviate sexual intercourse. The father died on October 5—a day before news broke that the lineman may be tried as an adult for some 26 felonies stemming from events that took place over several late nights in August at Mepham's football-training camp in Wayne County, Pennsylvania. Waiting outside in front of the hearse is a police escort, to ward off the media.

Relatives read from the books of Matthew and Wisdom. And then the lineman—whom classmates call a bully, who would shove kids he'd never even met into lockers as they walked by—stands suddenly, stepping out from his place in the front, and walks back eight rows to give a bear hug to his little brother, seated next to his mother (who was divorced from the father). The two boys join their sister to bring the Communion offerings forward as the mourners sing "Be Not Afraid."

And he stands where the priest stood and speaks, reading from crinkled sheets of paper rapidly, almost inaudibly, in a low monotone. "My father was a great man," he begins, and tells a story of how his dad once saw a crashed, burning car, pulled over and ran to help, and discovered that the guy trapped in the passenger's seat was a friend. His dad saved his friend's life that day. That, the lineman says, is the kind of man his father was.

During the recessional, he submits to a seemingly endless succession of embraces—much like the ones he received from his former teammates last night at the wake. He strokes his sister's hair with one hand and slides an arm around his brother's shoulders. He's the man of the family now.
• *Treat others with the respect that you would like to receive.*
• *Act appropriately. Know what is expected and acceptable.*
• *Be responsible. Expect to be held accountable for your choices and   actions.*
• *Be truthful. —From "The Mepham Way," Mepham High School's honor code*

48 MINUTES OF HELL, A LIFETIME TO REMEMBER —*Slogan on a Mepham Pirates football T-shirt*

In the southern reaches of Long Island, nestled between the bucolic Southern State Parkway and the fast-food joints and car dealerships on Sunrise Highway, the four small towns of Bellmore, North Bellmore, Merrick, and North Merrick make up a solid community of working- and middle-class families. These towns lost seventeen people in the World Trade Center attacks. They're places whose kids go to college locally and then settle here and raise families. Before last month, Mepham High was generally known as an above-average school with a robust

41

athletic program. Fathers and sons have played for the Mepham Pirates, and Saturday football games are huge social events. The players are the school's heroes: With the possible exception of Roone Arledge, Mepham's most famous alumnus has been star Pittsburgh Steelers running back Amos Zereoue. When people talked about Mepham, they talked about Famous Amos.

Now when they talk about Mepham, they use the words *sodomy* and *hazing*. They speak of broomsticks, pinecones, and golf balls.

The police call what happened in August at the Pirates' five-day training camp a series of Abner Louima–style sex attacks (though, curiously, no student interviewed by police has even mentioned Louima's name). They were carried out over several nights, with several victims, one of whom required surgery for his injuries. After the coaches went to sleep in their own cabin, at least three members of the team, ages 15, 16, and 17, allegedly rubbed heat-producing mineral ice on broomsticks, pinecones, and golf balls and used those items to penetrate at least three freshman players while the rest of the boys in the cabin all bore witness. The purported ringleader, according to police, was the lineman.

When the victims came forward, the team closed ranks. Kids who were said to have witnessed the attacks refused to talk, even though the longtime coach of the Pirates, Kevin McElroy—Coach Mac to anyone who knows him—warned them that the season would end if they didn't come forward. Instead, the victims were laughed at in the halls, called "faggot" and "broomstick boy." The superintendent, Thomas Caramore, shielded the school from inquiries at first. He told Pennsylvania police that he couldn't release information about a student without a subpoena. Nor did he suspend the three alleged perpetrators, and as a result, they were allowed to walk the hallways of Mepham High for nearly two weeks.

Throughout September, a question hung in the air: Would Wayne County district attorney Mark Zimmer try the boys as adults, which would mean that each could face up to twenty years in prison? On October 6, he announced that that was his intention. The lineman's father's death on October 5 created one delay in moving the case forward; other delays have been due to the attorneys' efforts to bring the case back to juvenile status, and to negotiate their clients' surrender into custody.

On September 17, the Bellmore-Merrick Central High School District Board of Education canceled Mepham's football season. A day later, the three boys were suspended, and a student demonstration erupted behind the school—to the delight of the TV crews camped out there. Days later, the school went ahead with its annual pep rally, in a gesture of support for Coach Mac and the sidelined Pirates.

"Most of the shit they did was *pranks,* like shaving cream," one Mepham boy tells me on a sunny Wednesday, a day before the funeral of the lineman's father. "Yeah, that shit got freakin' blown up. Half that shit they did isn't even that bad."

The boy, wearing a regulation backward baseball cap, is standing at the school's west entrance. He and a group of kids have me surrounded. Most of them are yelling. They're sick of reporters, and they're worried about the lineman.

"The kid that did it, I feel so *bad* for him," the boy says. "I don't even *care* what they did."

What about the boys who were raped? I ask.

"Two of the kids are underclassmen, little kids," he says. "They really couldn't do anything about it. But one kid who got it in the shitter, he's just like a *fag*."

He stops, waiting for my reaction.

"Yeah," he says. "I heard the kid *liked* it."

A day later, the three alleged victims are still having broomsticks thrown at them from cars in the parking lot. Some kids even approach them and suggest that the time has come to let bygones be bygones. Their logic is biblical—an eye for an eye. *The lineman's father died! Hasn't he been through enough?*

Sometimes it's hard to tell what bothers the people of Bellmore and Merrick more—allegations of sodomy or the abrupt end of football season. At a school-board meeting on October 1, packed with camera crews and angry parents, Superintendent Caramore tries to explain that hazing simply doesn't happen at Mepham—that football was canceled not because of what the boys allegedly did but because their teammates never reported it. That hasn't satisfied parents who complain about the lost scholarships, the deflated homecoming celebration, and the fund-raisers for other sports, all of which depend on football and are now ruined, they're saying, because of a couple of messed-up kids.

But other voices emerge at the meeting, corroborating the victims' contention that hazing is a fact of life at Mepham. Kristina and Vic Reichstein stand up and say their son, a freshman, was threatened by the lineman during practice in July and August. Another parent, Jim Rullo, delivers a prepared statement on behalf of the victims' families. He quotes one of the boys as saying, "I will never trust anyone again. They did not come to help me." Rullo quotes the parent of that child as blaming principal John Didden, who "did not protect my child.

Four days later, Rullo and two other parents who spoke receive identical profanity-laced letters in the mail, warning that if they keep speaking out, they'll also get the broomstick treatment. "Keep your mouth shut," the letters read, "and nothing will happen to you or your family."

Mepham was known mainly for its wrestling program until Coach Mac arrived in 1986. Then it became a football school. With Famous Amos on the squad, the team made the county playoffs all four years. McElroy was practically a second father to Zereoue when the running back moved to a home for wayward boys in Bellmore—arriving, to Mepham's good fortune, at the start of his high-school career. Amos scored 29 touchdowns in his junior year and broke all of Long Island's rushing records.

In recent years, the Pirates haven't done as well, losing roughly as many games as they've won, but the coach remains a local legend—a father figure who welcomes players to his house for barbecues with his teenage daughters in attendance. It's not surprising, then, that McElroy and the administration would be the first stop on the who's-to-blame tour. Parents demanded: Shouldn't they have been there to stop these boys?

The superintendent, while admonishing the team for not cooperating with the investigation, has also put forward a tidy defense of McElroy and the principal, Didden. Despite the lineman's threats, "no one could have anticipated" what happened at camp, Caramore told parents in a speech, adding that whatever happened wasn't hazing: "None of us in Bellmore-Merrick has used that term to define what is, in fact, a brutal crime."

The hazing-or-not debate is a key factor in the legal battles to come. Because if these attacks are accepted as hazing, then the school is responsible. Which may explain why Coach Mac, in his only public statement, has concurred with Caramore. "We as coaches do not see this incident as hazing," he said, "but as a criminal act."

Coach Mac has an attorney, Joseph Rosenthal, who is shifting the blame right back to the parents. "The coach is a very dedicated, sincere person," the lawyer says. "The coach went along with canceling the season because he knew kids were not coming forward. The problem was with the kids—and with the parents who brought them up that way."

So—the parents. The question has whirled around Bellmore for weeks: Who would raise a child who would do this to another child? Yet to place responsibility on any adult, coach or parent, means at least partially acquitting the kids; to suggest that someone should have stopped them is to believe that they could have been stopped. No one understands this better than Mark Alter, the lawyer for the alleged ringleader. "The fact that it's egregious allegations does not necessarily mean it's not a juvenile case," says Alter. He suggests that broomsticks, golf balls, and pinecones are consistent with traditional forms of hazing. He cites essays about hazing from the Internet, including an academic paper by Elizabeth Allan of the University of Maine that includes in a long list of hazing activities "sexual simulation and sexual assault."

"The conduct took place in a juvenile setting," Alter argues. "The fact that these studies show the prevalence of this

46

conduct in many hazing situations supports a conclusion that there's no reason to believe that this would have occurred outside of such a setting, or a belief that such conduct would reoccur."

Besides, he notes, "the juvenile-justice system affords kids a second chance. Weren't they already on the right track? After all, they weren't just students—they were athletes."

There's fury and finger-pointing—and opportunity—on all sides in this corner of Long Island.

"In my mind, the school made a major error in not suspending these three alleged perpetrators," says Robert Kelly, an attorney for two victims. "Ultimately, it's gonna be a civil case." Abner Louima sued the New York Police Department for $155 million, eventually settling for $8.75 million. If three victims get anything close to that much each, it would devastate the school district's budget.

Or as David Woycik, who represents another victim, puts it: "There's bound to be a movie made about this."

'This is not what I signed on for when I tried to do the right thing," says Vic Reichstein. "But I just got off the phone with the mother of one of the victims, and she told me that we're her best advocate. We're doing this so they don't have to."

In July, when Reichstein's son, an incoming freshman, showed up for football practice, a junior on the team—the lineman—started calling him and some of the other boys "pussy," "faggot," and "cocksucker." Reichstein went to McElroy. He says the coach said, "Okay, I'll handle it." From that moment on, the junior stopped calling Reichstein's son "faggot" and started calling him "tattletale boy."

One day at practice, the lineman approached him while he was drinking from a water fountain. "Who do you think you are?" said the lineman, according to Reichstein's son. "Are you on crack? Do you know who I am?"

The freshman, trying to show a little backbone, replied: "This is America. Go to the back of the line."

The lineman was furious. "Don't even think about sleeping at camp," he said.

Reichstein called Didden, whose reply, according to Reichstein, was that there was no hazing at Mepham, "because if there were, we'd cancel football season." (Didden and his attorney did not return repeated calls.) Reichstein's wife, Kristina, then begged Didden to make an example of the lineman. According to her, Didden said he would investigate the incident. "I'm the principal," he said, "and I'll decide who can go on the trip." The lineman was allowed to go to camp.

On a Friday morning in August, 60 kids were dropped off for the bus ride to Pennsylvania. Reichstein tried to stare the lineman down. He gave his son a cell phone. He told him to find a friend and never be alone.

"I told him what hazing was," he says. "I did not explain to him that hazing was golf balls, broomsticks, and pinecones." Reichstein's son was unharmed; three other freshmen weren't so lucky.

When parents came to an emergency meeting on September 16 with the principal and superintendent, they heard not mea culpas but accusations. "Due to the poor moral character of your children," Kristina says Caramore told the parents, "this investigation is not moving forward." She stood up and asked Didden twice if any child had been threatened before the camp incidents. She says Didden said no twice. That's when Vic stood up and called Didden a liar. Now the Reichsteins have written the state Department of Education, demanding an investigation.

Vic and Kristina have done The Early Show and 20/20. But they don't want to appear self-serving, he says.

"Not like Wesley Berger," Vic says. "He's overexposed."

In 1994, Wesley Berger was a Mepham freshman, a football player with a shelf of trophies—MVP for the peewee league, fastest-runner and best-tackler awards. He was dying to play for the Pirates—he'd gotten Amos Zereoue's autograph when Zereoue visited his junior high. That was until Berger started practice the August before his freshman year.

A player tried to flush his head in a urinal. He resisted, and according to his version of events, he remembers a JV coach telling him to roll with it.

Once the season started, eight players tackled him in the locker room and lowered him into the toilet; this time, he says, it contained urine. They hit his head on the porcelain and he got a concussion. Berger says he got up and called his dad, who went straight to the coaches. Then came the civil suit, settled for a paltry sum, to cover medical bills. Berger got threatening letters: "Keep singing, Berger, and you'll see."

He was benched for two years as the lawsuit crept through the legal system. "I was by far the best halfback on the team," Berger says, now 23 but still angry. "There's no way you can't play me. In practice, they'd put me on the B squad and I'd tear up the A squad." He says he stayed on the team for two years but was allowed on the field only once, returning a kickoff 50 yards.

49

"Everybody knew I got hazed in the locker room," he says. "I said, 'You want to lock me in a locker and laugh for an hour, fine. But I'm not down with urine, dude.' "

At the beginning of his junior year, Berger says, he showed up to start the season. The coach told Berger he needed a physical. Berger produced the required slip of paper. He says the coach started yelling. "He's like, 'No! No! *No!!!* Effin' this, effin' that— you're not coming on my team, you're done, you're done, you're done!' And I started screaming at him."

That's when Berger says Coach Mac lunged at him—his hand reaching the boy's throat.

"The guy grabbed me in front of the whole team," Berger says. "This is hard to say—I know he was a good coach and a lot of kids liked him. But it really happened."

McElroy's lawyer vehemently denies almost every aspect of Berger's story. "McElroy had nothing to do with this kid," Joe Rosenthal says. "What I know about the Berger incident is it did not involve hazing. It involved a fight among teenage boys. He never brought this incident to McElroy's attention; he must have brought it to the JV coach's attention. And McElroy never prevented him from playing on the varsity team. Any player that wants to be on the football team can be on the team. There's a no-cut policy. You may not *start*, but you'll be on the team."

Berger says his friends persuaded him to stay off the team. He wrestled instead. But he wonders whether what happened at camp could have been prevented if he hadn't settled his lawsuit.

"Of *course* this thing escalated to sodomy," Berger says. "This guy's still the head coach."

It's a fact of life in Bellmore and Merrick that the farther south you go, the more money you'll find. Mepham's student body is pulled from the northern part of the community, where there are $50,000-a-year jobs and the school parking lot is dominated by Chevys and Fords. A few miles away—south of Sunrise Highway, down by the blue water of East Bay—BMWs and Lexuses fill the lot at the rival high school, John F. Kennedy. This was Amy Fisher's high school—the rich school. Says one Mepham parent, "We're always in competition with the upper class."

The kids on Kennedy's football team know the Mepham team, and they're a little afraid of some of them. One afternoon after practice, they air their theories, the chief one being that the lineman must have been traumatized as a kid. "That kid was *sick!*" says a player named Rob. Does he know this for sure? Of course not. But it's not the only time I hear neighbors, even parents, float this notion. (Almost as prevalent is the idea, not confirmed by police, that the lineman's father committed suicide.)

"I knew *all* those kids," says another boy, a JV player. "I went to summer school with them." The lineman, he says, "was always starting fights. You could just see he had so much anger in him. He'd just beat up on people—he'd be walking by and *boom!* Into the locker! I think he's a dirtbag. Decent football player, though."

"The morals, the attitudes, of a Mepham student, are different," suggests another Kennedy player, Danny.

Adds Jesse: "Mepham kids say, 'You're from Kennedy,' and punch us. They're the bully school, the physical school. Even in middle school, we knew which kids were going to Mepham and which to Kennedy."

"We're more Jewish!" another kid yells, laughing.

"We have more wealthy backgrounds," says Danny.

"They're big football players who look and act like football players," says Jesse. "Big and aggressive."

The lineman "was yelled at a lot," remembers another boy. "He was always in trouble at school, but not in football. Sports in Mepham is *very* big."

What's Kennedy's record?

"We've been 0 and 8 since 1999!" says James.

On Bellmore Avenue, the main drag in town, a mile or so east of Mepham, Doc's Pub serves as an unofficial class-reunion space. It's the kind of bar where people still smoke and no one cares. On a warm night in October, Mary Williams and her boyfriend, Andy Corcoran, both Mepham class of 1980, sit having a drink. Mary is a third-generation "Bellmoron." Her boy, Kyle, played varsity. He went to camp but didn't stay in the fated cabin. "He knows the main kid," she says. "He's been in trouble before, that kid. He's well known as a bully. But my son says nobody knew he would cross the line."

Andy's son plays lacrosse. This is a sore point for Mary. "Your son—*woo hoo!* He's having fun. My son's not. He doesn't have a senior season to put on his college application."

"This guy comes to my job," says Andy. "He says, 'Oh, I'm in *Mepham* now, maybe I should shove a pinecone up my ass!' I said, 'That's not funny.' These guys on the team are gonna be harassed the rest of their fuckin' lives."

"My son knows one of the boys who was attacked," Mary says sadly. "He tried seriously to treat him as a regular kid, like nothing ever happened. And I know the family of one of the attackers. They're a beautiful family. My son thinks it's just a bad thing that went too far, too fast."

Andy mentions what some people are saying—that what happened at camp was part of a pattern of hazing at Mepham. Mary explodes. "Who? *Wesley?* Wesley was a nasty rat bastard! That was *hazing!* This was a sexual attack!"

"Yeah," says Andy, "but—"

"Are we gonna argue about this? My son's season has been completely fucked up! His friend was a captain on the team, he maybe was gonna get a scholarship. Who's going to give him that money now? I think the kids covered it up to save Coach Mac and save their season."

Tending bar at Doc's is Rob McDermott, class of '95. He was one of four captains chosen by Coach Mac his senior season. "A captain is an extension of the coaching staff," he says, slipping into present tense to talk about his team. "What the coaches don't control, the captains control. Whether it's being in the locker room, making sure everybody's on the same page, rallying the troops, or making sure everyone's focused on the task at hand."

How do you weed out the undisciplined players? "On any high-school team, the seniors give you a little bit of a hard time," he says. "We built a very good tradition with our team, and we just want to make sure that anyone who wants to fit in on the team knows about the tradition."

What about, say, having your head flushed in a toilet?

"It's all fun and games," says McDermott. "And coming in, you expect it. You're ready for it."

Was Wesley Berger expecting it?

53

"From what I heard, the guys stuck his head in the toilet, and that was it. We don't beat guys up."

Some of his old teammates have gathered to buy drinks from him. The conversation easily shifts to a defense of Coach Mac. "He never judged us," says Dave Lohman, class of '94. "He always listened. He did more for me than any coach ever. And because we were the group with Amos, our team is etched in his memory."

"The coaches would have to be everywhere at the same time," says Dave Hill.

"When I was in ninth grade," says Lohman, "my father died and my mother wanted to move to Florida. Coach Mac talked to my mom, convinced us to stay. He taught us not to run away from our problems."

"How old were these kids, 16, 17?" says Andrew Longaro. "You're old enough to know what you're doing."

So, I ask, were any of you guys flushed?

"I had some friends who were older," says McDermott. "So, no."

The others also shake their heads no.

"But, you know," says McDermott, "if they wanted to do it? Go ahead. I want to be part of the team."

. . .

3 Robert Kolker. "Out of Bounds", NYMAG.COM. 2003

In the North High case, coach John Torno was placed on paid administrative leave, but police said he was not investigated for any criminal wrongdoing.

According to police, the four students assaulted another boy Dec. 19 at the high school. The incident was reported to police Jan. 3, after holiday break.

Sioux City Police Lt. Rex Mueller said the incident appeared to involve humiliation techniques on bare skin of sensitive body parts of the 15-year-old victim. Two 18-year-olds, a 17-year-old and a 16-year-old were cited with simple assault, a misdemeanor, in connection with the incident, he said.

Sioux City schools spokeswoman Alison Benson said the incident occurred in the locker room at North. She would not provide specific details about the allegations, citing school policy protecting student disciplinary records, but confirmed all five students were on the wrestling team.

School officials have spoken with the team about the incident and disciplined the students in accordance with school policy, Benson said.

"We've addressed it, and I can't comment on what occurred," she said.

Torno, of Sioux City, was put on paid administrative leave while school officials investigated the incident, Benson said.

"Our investigation is complete and he will be back in the classroom" today, she said.

She would not comment on whether Torno, who will also resume coaching duties, was disciplined as a result of the investigation. Contacted Wednesday, Torno said he did not want talk about the allegations.

A similar incident occurred in south-central Iowa the same day as the incident at North.

Two members of the wrestling team at Nodaway High School in Greenfield have been arrested on charges of second-degree sexual abuse in an alleged hazing incident, police said Wednesday. They said an assault occurred Dec. 19 in the high school's wrestling room and that two other students might have been victims of similar attacks.

In late December, authorities said several Lisbon High School students were punished for bullying and harassment after a student on the eastern Iowa school's wrestling team reported being hazed. The Linn County attorney is considering charges in that case.

. . .

4 Montag Molly. "North high wrestlers charges in hazing incident." *Sioux City Journal*. 12 January 2012.

Sioux City Iowa – follow up[5]:

A North High School wrestler has been placed on probation for participating in the December assault of a teammate.

Alberto Jurado, 17, of Sioux City, was placed on probation for one year after admitting to a charge of aiding and abetting assault. The closed hearing was held in Woodbury County Juvenile Court on Thursday.

In a ruling filed Monday, Juvenile Judge Mary Timko ordered Alberto to comply with the terms of a consent decree, which requires him to write a letter of apology to the victim, write a three-page essay on the topic of "The Dangers of Hazing Behaviors" and complete 40 hours of community service.

Alberto's brother, Angel Jurado, 16, also will admit to aiding and abetting assault. He has requested a consent decree, and a hearing is set for May 3.

According to court documents, four boys on Dec. 19 grabbed the 15-year-old victim in a school locker room and pulled his pants down. While the victim was held down, his buttocks were spread and sprayed with lotion, the court papers allege.

The other two wrestlers were charged in Woodbury County District Court. Peter Stewart and Nathan Calvillo, both 18, have each pleaded guilty to simple assault. They received a deferred judgment and were ordered to pay a $65 civil penalty. Stewart must complete 25 hours of community service, and Calvillo must finish 40 hours.

Three other Iowa school districts have dealt with abusive behavior in their wrestling programs this winter. Incidents have been investigated at Nodaway Valley, Lisbon and Gilbert.

. . .

5   Hytrek, Nick. " Wrestler gets probation in North High School locker room assault." *Sioux City Journal*. 12 March 2012.

The incident is said to involve several members of the Nodaway Valley High School wrestling team.

KCCI News talked exclusively with a former member of that team who says he quit out of fear he too would be sexually assaulted.

The Nodaway Valley High School student, who didn't want us to show his face, says he recently quit the wrestling team out of fear that he would be sexually assaulted by other members, something he saw happen to other teammates.

"They threatened to do it to me if I missed another practice, so I didn't go back to practice, and I kind of quit," said the student.

Greenfield police say an incident happened in late December at Nodaway Valley High School. Besides the fact that they are investigating, and that it involves several students, police won't reveal much more.

Greenfield residents told KCCI the attack happened in the locker room. They said several members of the school's wrestling team allegedly held down a 16-year-old teammate and sexually assaulted him as a punishment for missing practice.

"I was kind of scared because I was thinking if I did quit they could catch me after school or something and do it," said the student.

He says it became common for senior members of the team to punish a younger wrestler if he didn't make weight or missed practice by holding him down and shoving a jump rope up his rear end.

"There were some people who were kind of for it, so they would hold you down, and someone else would stick it up your butt as they pulled your shorts down," said the student.

While officials are remaining tight-lipped, there is mixed reaction around town. Some people told KCCI they are glad the story is out there because they are upset about what happened. While others said they'd rather it remained quiet.

"You don't hear about it much just because you don't want to talk about it," said the student.

There was no one at the police station when KCCI sought comment. KCCI News also knocked on the Police Chief's front door hoping to get a police report or any more information. He refused to give us any information and kicked us off his property.

KCCI News also talked with the school's superintendent, Casy Berlau, who says the school is conducting its own investigation but would not reveal if anyone has been suspended or expelled.

. . .

6 "Former High School Wrestler Talks About Hazing Incident". KCCI TV. 9 January 2012.

Two Andover High students have been expelled and at least five others kicked off the basketball team for their roles in a "disturbing" case of hazing against two underclassmen at a basketball camp last July, sources have confirmed.

The punishments may not end there. Sources confirm the Bristol County District Attorney's office will pursue criminal charges and the state Attorney General's office has launched its own investigation.

Nine Andover High players attended the Hoop Mountain basketball camp at Stonehill College in Easton, Mass., where the incident occurred. The Eagle-Tribune reported older students forced two underclassmen to play a humiliating sex game known as "wet biscuit," where the loser was made to eat a semen-covered cookie.

The two ringleaders of the hazing were expelled while the others involved received suspensions for an unknown amount of time and will not be allowed to compete in school sports for the remainder of the school year, sources said.

In a letter sent Wednesday to parents, Superintendent Marinel McGrath said her investigation confirmed students violated the schools' anti-hazing and anti-bullying policies, and called the players' actions "both disappointing and disturbing."

However, she refused to say what punishments were meted out.

"While I fully understand and appreciate that you are legitimately interested in the outcomes for the violations of these policies, I am prohibited by federal and state laws from disclosing information about individual student discipline," McGrath wrote. "I can tell you, however, that in the case of violations of our anti-bullying and anti-hazing policies, our school district policies permit a range of disciplinary actions which include suspension and expulsion from school."

Andover High Athletic Director Christopher Bergeron also did not specify how many players were punished or how. In his letter to parents, he wrote he "intends" to suspend team members involved for "varying period of time due to apparent violations of Andover High School athletic policies and rules.

"As stated in the rules, which apply to all athletic programs, participation in the AHS Athletic Program is a privilege, not a right, and the highest standards of conduct will be enforced," Bergeron wrote.

McGrath's letter also states, "We will address, separately, the involvement of any Andover Public Schools employees in connection with these allegations."

David Fazio, coach of the Andover High boys' basketball team, refused to comment for this story. Fazio also works as a physical education teacher at the school.

Fazio learned of the hazing incident Nov. 11 and reported the incident to police and school officials. Sources said Fazio helped the boy who ate the cookie tell his parents, and then organized a meeting with them and the ringleaders and their parents.

The other boy pressured into playing the game has since left the Andover school district.

Fazio's lawyer Michael Morris previously stated his client "acted promptly, compassionately, professionally, legally and morally by responding to the boy and his parents, some of the parents of other boys involved, to the Andover Police and his superiors all at the first opportunity."

Andover Police are helping Easton Police — located in Bristol County — with the investigation. Andover police Lt. James Hashem said last night the incident remains under investigation. A call to the Easton Police Department was not returned.

Those convicted of hazing face up to a year in jail and a $3,000 fine. Anyone who witnesses hazing but does not report it faces a $1,000 fine if convicted under state law.

McGrath has not commented publicly on the incident, except for her letters to parents. School Committee Chairwoman Annie Gilbert said McGrath briefed the committee during a closed-door executive session shortly after the allegations surfaced.

"I have full faith in the process the superintendent has conducted, and I have every confidence that she made her decisions with the best intentions of the students and the community in mind," Gilbert said last night.

. . .

7 Putnam Gretchen and Brian Messenger. "Two 'hazing' players expelled, 5 others booted from Andover hoop team." *Gloucester Times*. 1 December 11.

COLLEGE HAZING

Virtually every school in America has a written policy against hazing. Yet 80% of student-athletes are subjected to it. So stricter policies are not necessarily the answer.

As Dr. Amber Warner's research on leadership and alcohol so clearly demonstrates (see link below), student-athletes actual behaviors are most influenced by the attitudes and actions of the team leaders, rather than the policies of the school or the frequency of admonitions from coaches.

Plain and simple, if the leaders use and abuse alcohol, the team members take their cues from them and follow suit. If the leaders take a responsible approach to alcohol, the teammates do as well.

This finding can likely be applied to hazing as well. Your leaders are the key people when it comes to determining how your veteran athletes will "welcome" the freshmen on the team. If your leaders believe initiation ceremonies are okay, you've got a recipe for disaster and must act quickly.

If your leaders believe that hazing is not the thing to do and dissuade other teammates from doing so, you have your best insurance policy against it.

Thus, as usual, the leaders are the key. And working with them and through them is your job as the coach.

CASE HISTORY 1 8
Bloomington, Ill.

Despite Illinois Wesleyan University's attempts over the years to put an end to hazing, both allegations and instances of hazing practiced by fraternities and sororities are emerging this semester.

At the request of all eight victims/witnesses of hazing The Argus interviewed for its investigation, names (both of individuals and organizations), class years and genders have been omitted. Sources feared severe harassment and bullying should their identities be discovered.

One Greek organization member recalled an event in which fraternity members were stripped naked and told to run around school grounds. "I just looked away, I felt embarrassed for them," the source said.

Further allegations include pressured and/or forced underage drinking.

Sources willing to speak with The Argus expressed a sense of betrayal and disappointment in response to the hazing. "They promised me they were never going to haze us," one of the sources said, "our campus even has an anti-hazing week."

A number of sources were willing to share more detailed accounts of their hazing experience several years in the past. Still, they wished to remain anonymous.

"On initiation night, we had to sit on the floor in the doorways of separate rooms, writing about why we wanted to join the sorority and why we deserved to be in it," one alumni source said. "The whole time, the senior girls were walking around screaming at us and slamming paddles on the door frames and walls right above our heads."

"One girl started laughing so they put her in the shower and turned the water on her fully clothed, even though we were all dressed up in formalwear for initiation. We weren't allowed to stop writing for a long time. Finally they took us downstairs blindfolded, and made us sit at tables in a dark room."

A second source also shared her experience. "[During a hazing event] they would yell questions at us about [the Greek organization's] history that we were supposed to have memorized, and if you got it wrong, they would yell about how you were unworthy to be a [member of the Greek organization]."

"I was so pissed off that we were being screamed at, I thought it was such bullshit," the second source said.

When asked about hazing's effect on their perception of fraternities and sororities, one current student source who pledged this semester said, "Being in Greek life made me lose my self-worth, and I'm not ok with that." This student deactivated from the organization following a hazing incident.

"Initiation night was pretty humiliating. I feel embarrassed looking back on it, thinking about how I allowed myself to be so emotionally degraded by anyone, let alone girls who claimed to become my 'sisters' once the process was over," a source said.

"Your real friends would never do anything that makes you feel like you need to suffer—physically, psychologically, mentally, whatever—in order to deserve their respect."

After witnessing an unsettling hazing incident, a member of a Greek organization said, "It's a mindset on our campus. The perpetrators, victims, and Greek life just accept it."

The same source recounted feelings about their own experience being hazed. "I was never in physical danger," said the source. "But looking back, there are things I'm surprised I didn't protest against. There were things happening that were against my beliefs, but I didn't say anything at the time. And that's the scary part."

Some officials within Greek life commented on the allegations of hazing on campus.

"You always hope that nothing is going on, but you never really know," said a fraternity leader who wished to remain anonymous.

"Panhellenic takes hazing very seriously and all of our policies on the issue are available online" said Mary Heath, the College Panhellenic Council vice-president of administration.

Some sources reflect these Greek life members' sentiment concerning hazing. "Some of the older ones apologized to us and said it would never happen again. They're taking steps to make it stop," a source said.

Illinois Wesleyan administration has taken a firm stance on hazing, attempting to stop further incidents from happening this year.

"Hazing is not just something that happens in Greek Life," said Blake Bradley, Director of Fraternity and Sorority Life at IWU. "It happens in many other organizations as well, and everyone handles it in different ways. You can have 30 people in a pledge class getting hazed and everyone will be affected differently. No one can know what that person has been through in their life or how hazing can impact them."

"Hazing can refer to a wide variety of things, but it's basically anything a pledge is forced to do or go through that a full member would not have to do," said Vice-President and Dean of Students Karla Carney-Hall. "I generally refer to incidents as being either 'little h' hazing or 'big H' Hazing."

Little h "hazing," according to Carney-Hall, could consist of active members making pledges answer phones or emails for them. Big H "Hazing" is what people generally associate with the term: forced drinking, humiliation, psychological or physical abuse, etc.

Carney-Hall says there have been four instances of hazing reported and investigated by the university administration since she came to Illinois Wesleyan in 2011. But this has not shaken her belief in fraternities and sororities on campus.

"Fraternity and sorority leaders on campus have offered 100 percent cooperation and integrity in taking responsibility and making efforts to address [hazing]," Carney-Hall said. She referred to the 250 Greek students who went through "bystander training" this fall—meant to teach students how to deal with and report unethical behavior within their organizations—as evidence of their efforts.[i]

---

i ANNA LOWENTHAL, "Students' hazing experiences on IWU campus come to light: Greek leaders respond to controversy." *The Argus*. 16 November 2012.

CASE HISTORY 2 [9]
Knoxville, Tenn

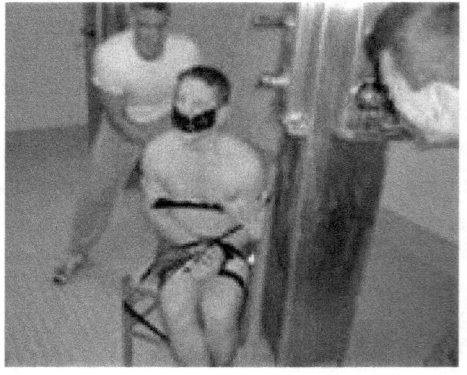

The University of Tennessee says it has suspended a fraternity chapter indefinitely and may refocus its alcohol education programs after police said a student was hospitalized following a weekend incident involving alcohol enemas.

Twelve Tennessee students were cited with underage drinking and one with disorderly conduct following the incident early Saturday at a Pi Kappa Alpha fraternity chapter house, according to a university spokeswoman.

"Shock would not be an (overstatement)," Tim Rogers, vice chancellor of student life, told reporters Wednesday. "I myself had never heard of what has been alleged."

Knoxville police say they began investigating after a student was taken to the UT Medical Center in critical condition early Saturday with a blood alcohol level of 0.40 -- five times the legal cutoff for driving.

Experts: Alcohol enemas 'extremely dangerous'

"Upon extensive questioning, it is believed that members of the fraternity were using rubber tubing inserted into their rectums as a conduit for alcohol as the abundance of capillaries and blood vessels present greatly heightens the level and speed of the alcohol entering the bloodstream as it bypasses the filtering by the liver," Knoxville Police spokesman Darrell DeBusk said Monday in a statement. The student has been released, the hospital said. Initial reports released by the UT Police Department on Wednesday indicated that the student's cousin -- a UT student and Pi Kappa Alpha member who says he wasn't at the house that night -- told investigators that the hospitalized student had used an alcohol enema. However, the student's parents say their son denies involvement and that the cousin is willing to sign an affidavit saying he didn't make that statement to police. DeBusk said he is standing by his account.
"It was information gathered through the course of our investigation, which has now been turned over to the UT Police Department," he said. Knoxville police said investigators found tubing and materials used to give alcohol enemas at the scene. They also said a witness told them that the hospitalized student had used an alcohol enema. Is underage drinking ever OK?

Reports released by UT police Wednesday say investigators saw beer cans and bottles and "bags from wine boxes, some empty and some partially empty, strewn across the halls and rooms."
UT spokeswoman Karen Simsen said that hazing does not appear to have been involved. "It's just an incident involving alcohol," she said. Rogers said the university has suspended the chapter indefinitely "until we wrap up this investigation." He cautioned that the university considers the enema reports to be only allegations, and that neither police nor the university has

70

completed investigations. He said the incident came only a week or two after campus officials met with UT fraternity and sorority student leaders about alcohol. The university, which generally forbids alcohol on campus, has anti-alcohol-abuse efforts, including unannounced checks of common areas in residence halls.

The school also offers programs showing that, according to research, "students think that other students drink much more than they do," and therefore "you don't need to go out there and try to keep up," Rogers said. "We're going to continue the education, we're going to continue the walk throughs," he said. "We don't have a lot of knee-jerk reactive initiatives. We want to fall back and maybe refocus on our existing programs."
The university will investigate the incident, and students could face university disciplinary action, Rogers said.

The Pi Kappa Alpha International Fraternity said it was investigating the incident. "The recent allegations against these individuals have come as a complete shock to The Pi Kappa Alpha International Fraternity, its 15,000 undergraduate members and over 200,000 living alumni, family and friends," the statement said. "Pi Kappa Alpha's mission is to develop men of integrity, intellect and high moral character and to foster a truly lifelong fraternal experience. These alleged activities are clearly not consistent with that mission, nor are they representative of what the fraternity would expect from any of its members."

The fraternity office said it put its own suspension on the chapter, set to last 30 days or until a decision is made regarding the long-term status of the chapter. According to the National Institute on Alcohol Abuse and Alcoholism, 1,825 college students between the ages of 18 and 24 die each year from alcohol-related unintentional injuries.

71

Aaron White, a health scientist administrator at the National Institute on Alcohol Abuse and Alcoholism, said he knows of several stories in the past year or so "about young people finding unique ways to get alcohol in their bodies." But he said they seem to be fairly isolated incidents.

"This is extraordinarily dangerous, but people shouldn't get the impression that it's a widespread phenomenon," White said.

. . .

9 CNN Wire Staff "Tennessee fraternity suspended after alcohol enemas" 27 September 2012

CASE HISTORY 3 [10]
AMES, IOWA

Sigma Alpha Epsilon's national headquarters has closed its 107-year-old chapter at the University of Iowa, one of the longest-standing fraternities at UI, because of hazing.

The national organization said in a news release Monday that it has suspended the charter of its Iowa Beta chapter and expelled its members from the fraternity for failure to comply with its governing laws.

The nature of the hazing is unclear, though UI in a statement Monday said it "does not tolerate hazing or unsafe and illegal consumption of alcohol in any of its student organizations."

The Iowa City Press-Citizen reports SAE's headquarters will close the Manville Heights chapter house at 302 Ridgeland Ave., and its members will be required to move out, the organization said.

"Sigma Alpha Epsilon's board of directors will not tolerate hazing or behavior that violates risk-management policies or the general guidelines for chapter operations," the organization said in a news release. "The organization expects its chapters to adhere to stringent policies and practices that help our members become gentlemen and leaders, and to live up to our creed and principles."

UI student Mike Weaver, president of the Iowa Beta chapter, declined to comment.

The closure comes just five days after the SAE's headquarters announced it had suspended several members of its Gamma Chapter at Iowa State University for unspecified violations.

UI said Monday it fully supports the closure of the chapter and that it is investigating individual violations of its student life code.

"We are fortunate to have a strong and vibrant Greek community at the University of Iowa, which collectively plays an active role in community service and significant philanthropic efforts," UI said in a news release. "This incident is an aberration and perversion of the values that hundreds of fraternity and sorority members work hard to uphold, and should not reflect on the larger community of outstanding Greek students that contribute so much to our campus environment."

The Iowa City chapter house, located on the west side of the Iowa River a block off the intersection of Park Road and Riverside Drive, is owned by a private house corporation, the Iowa Beta Riverside Corporation, according to the Iowa City assessor website. The fraternity opened in 1905, according to the chapter's website before it was taken offline late Monday.

UI said that the fraternity members will be personally responsible for relocating because they independently had entered into a private housing arrangement with SAE. The university, however, said its student life office had resources available to assist members find off-campus housing options. No UI-owned housing space currently is available.

SAE's headquarters said the closure won't permanently cut the fraternity's ties with UI.

"We view the relationship with the University of Iowa as a partnership, and we hope to return to the campus in the future," the SAE national headquarters said in its statement.

UI's student conduct code states that alcoholic beverages may not be purchased or served at events sponsored by a student organization.

. . .

10   "University Of Iowa Fraternity Sigma Alpha Epsilon Shut Down Over Hazing"
The Des Moines Register. 26 September 2012

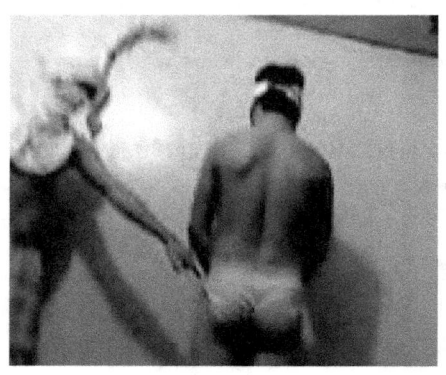

Despite prevention efforts, hazing persists on campuses

After the beating death, in 2011, of Florida A&M University drum major Robert Champion, Champion's parents did what other parents have done when faced with a similar loss.

They grieved. They sued. They started a non-profit foundation as a memorial to their son. Its mission: to "eradicate hazing nationwide."

They have their work cut out for them. Their son's death may have heightened the nation's awareness of the dangers and pervasiveness of college hazing, but it hasn't stopped risky behavior among students:

Police are investigating whether a Fresno (Calif.) State University student who died in August was participating in an alcohol-infused fraternity initiation.

At Chico State University, where a student died in a hazing incident seven years ago and a student was found dead last week after a night of drinking, the school has suspended Greek activities for the rest of the year, noting problems involving allegations of hazing, sexual assaults and drinking.

Ten members of Texas Southern University's renowned Ocean of Soul marching band were suspended this fall for paddling new members.

At the State University of New York-Geneseo, where the 2009 alcohol-related death of a student was attributed to hazing, freshmen on the women's volleyball team were handcuffed, blindfolded and forced to drink hard liquor, court documents allege. Campus officials suspended the women's volleyball team for the season and eight of 11 students charged with hazing and other misdemeanors accepted a plea agreement last week. A judge described the women's actions "premeditated, abusive, degrading and life-threatening."

Hazing is illegal in 44 states. College administrations don't condone it. And most student organizations have anti-hazing policies on the books. So why is it so persistent?

Anti-hazing activists cite a host of contributing factors, including the secretive nature of hazing, difficult-to-enforce state laws and an acceptance among many students that hazing is part of campus life.

"There's a new crop of students every four years who don't really remember the way things were," says Cornell University student Daniel Robbins. He helped organize a campus student newspaper-sponsored discussion held last week — the same day, as it happened, that the paper reported school officials were investigating allegations that two fraternity pledges who had been hospitalized were involved in hazing.

Hazing — and binge drinking, a related problem — has roiled the Ithaca, N.Y., campus since last year, when sophomore George Desdunes died in a fraternity hazing. Even before then, Cornell officials had prided themselves on their proactive approach to hazing, which included a website where hazing violations are posted publicly and students could report hazing incidents.

"Given our best efforts, we still had a death," says Travis Apgar, Cornell's associate dean of students.

Since then, a task force has developed recommendations, which have not yet been approved, to prevent hazing and enforce anti-hazing policies. For example, it calls for live-in advisers at more fraternity houses, incentives focused on academic excellence and random interviews with newly recruited students.

Other colleges, including Yale and Dartmouth, have similarly vowed to toughen up their efforts, typically in response to a recent tragedy or high-profile incident. At Binghamton

University in New York, officials last spring took the unusual step of shutting down fraternity and sorority recruitment after receiving what they called "an alarmingly high number of serious hazing complaints." E-mails obtained by the Binghamton Press & Sun-Bulletin describe reports in which students were forced to vomit on each other, made to do push ups on broken glass or engage in dangerous drinking games.

While hazing is typically associated with fraternity pledging, Champion's death underscored a growing body of evidence showing that hazing hardly ends with the Greek system. Of more than 11,000 college students nationwide surveyed in a landmark 2008 study, 55% of those students involved in clubs, teams or other organizations had experienced hazing as part of an initiation, and 47% said they had been hazed in high school.

Researchers are now linking hazing to high school bullying, says University of Maine professor Elizabeth Allan, co-author of the 2008 study and co-founder of the National Collaborative for Hazing Research and Prevention.

Allan, who served on a Florida A&M University (FAMU) anti-hazing task force, is cautiously hopeful that students and campus officials are no longer dismissing hazing as mostly silly pranks that sometimes go too far.

"It used to be that people would bring in a speaker or have a workshop on hazing and then they'd move on to the next issue," Allan says. "There is a greater commitment than ever before and we just hope that it can be sustained."

FAMU interim President Larry Robinson agrees, adding that it will take time to change the culture. "We're preparing to fight the long battle," he says.

Changes this fall include a requirement that all students take an anti-hazing pledge, and a new website where students can report suspicious behavior. At least four student groups, including two dance groups, a fraternity for business majors and a sorority for health-care majors, have been investigated based on tips — a sign to Robinson that awareness is up.

All were eventually cleared. Some of the reported activities, such as being forced to stand in place for long periods of time, did not meet state statutory requirements for criminal behavior, police statements show. In one case, the police were unable to identify a suspect or victim.

Hank Nuwer, a professor at Franklin College in Indiana who has written several books on the topic, worries that crackdowns could drive criminal behavior underground. He wants colleges to be more forthcoming, but says many, wary of lawsuits, are reluctant to draw attention to problems on their campuses.

"If the parents do not press it, the school will be happy to have it go away," says Nuwer, who keeps a running tab of hazing deaths based on news accounts.

By his count, at least one student has died every year in a hazing-related incident since 1970, and about 80% of them involve alcohol.

Nobody knows exactly how prevalent hazing on campuses because nobody is required to keep track. A small but growing number of campuses are posting details but that's not enough, Nuwer and others say.

"You can't start (fixing the problem) unless you start getting open disclosure about the problem around the country," says Washington lawyer Douglas Fierberg, who has represented numerous parents of children who died as a result of a hazing. "Everyone is left talking about an elusive problem without having access to the factual information."

. . .

Mary Beth Marklein. "Despite prevention efforts, hazing persists on campuses." *USA TODAY.* 20 November 2012.

CASE HISTORY 4 [11]
Albany, New York

Seven University at Albany students forced pledges to lie face down in a basement filled with water and then beat them with rubber hoses and paddles while demanding they beg "for mercy," police said.

The students who poured water over the heads of the prone pledges now face charges of hazing, a violation, and the possibility of discipline from the university, authorities said. Police said it appeared to be some kind of initiation from an underground fraternity or other organization not recognized by the university. The arrested students hosed down and beat pledges inside 470 Hudson Ave., Officer Steve Smith of the city police force said.

At 1:15 a.m. Friday, police found 14 young men lying face down on a flooded basement floor with their faces submerged, Smith said.

The group had run a hose in the basement and a few inches of water had collected, he said.

Police said the following residents of 470 Hudson Ave. were charged with hazing, criminal nuisance and unlawful assembly: John Storte, 19; Nicholas Salamone, 20; Joseph Lane, 20; and Anthony Morello, 20.

The following people were charged with hazing and unlawful assembly: Vincent Serrecchia, 20, of 487 Hudson Ave.; Joseph Sheehan, 21, of 489 Hudson Ave.; and Anthony Warme, 20, of the Bronx.

Police said Philip Terra, 21, was charged with obstruction of governmental administration and resisting arrest after he pushed an officer in an attempt to get inside the house.

One of the victims, Frank Calandra, 18, had prescription narcotics on him and was charged with criminal possession of a controlled substance. Some of the students had minor cuts and abrasions but refused medical attention. Fire investigators called to the scene found more than a dozen violations at the home. U Albany spokesman Karl Luntta confirmed that eight of those arrested were students. In a brief statement, he said none of the arrested or their victims were members of a recognized University at Albany fraternity. "U Albany is taking immediate action against those involved in this off-campus incident through the campus judicial disciplinary process," he said. "U Albany proactively educates students and parents about hazing issues and has a zero-tolerance policy for any actions that are physically and mentally abusive to the well-being of another." U Albany has more than 40 sanctioned fraternities and sororities, including some in the so-called "student ghetto" of Albany. U Albany monitors non-sanctioned fraternities and sororities and warns students that is a violation of the school's code of conduct to join one, said Michael Jaromin, the school's director of student involvement and leadership. He said the groups don't exhibit any of the positives of Greek life, like philanthropy, community service or connection to a national organization; they essentially exist just to chug beer.

81

"I just call them 'groups of guys,'" he said. "They may want to behave like a fraternity, but they don't have the behavior of a fraternity." Jaromin said the school has an anonymous hazing tip line that investigates every claim. This incident was the most serious in recent memory, he said.

While hazing has led to deaths at other schools around the country, it is rare in the State University of New York system because fraternities and sororities do not make up as significant a part of the student population as they do at other schools. Binghamton University suspended pledging at all of its fraternities and sororities last spring because school officials received numerous hazing complaints.

. . .

11 Waldman Scott.. "UAlbany Students accused of hazing". *Timesunion.com.* 12 November 2012

CASE HISTORY 5 [12]
Fort Worth, TX

Most college students returned for the spring semester rested and relaxed. Amon Carter IV headed back to class with the mark of his fraternity burned into his backside.

The family of Texas Christian University student, who returned from a winter break ski trip with second and third-degree burns from being branded by his fraternity brothers, have already hired a lawyer to pressure school officials and police to punish all involved.

Carter, who goes by Chance, will require surgery to repair the damage done to his buttocks with a hot coat hanger after he passed out during a night of drinking.

"Kids get drunk and do really stupid things," Carter's cousin Sheila Johnson told ABCNews.com. "This crossed the line."

Forth Worth lawyer Kathryn Craven told ABCNews.com she was hired by Chance Carter's father, Amon Carter III, after his son came home and showed his father the wounds.

"He wants the people who did this to be held accountable under every possible entity because this was a torturous act," she said.

The branding allegedly took place on Jan. 9, when members of the Kappa Sigma fraternity and the Tri Delta sorority were on vacation in Breckenridge, Colo.

WFAA

Texas Christian University student Amon Carter IV returned from a winter break ski trip with third-degree burns from being branded by his fraternity brothers.

Johnson, who is close to the TCU sophomore, told ABCNews.com that Chance Carter had drunkenly consented to letting his fraternity brothers finish branding his rear with the Kappa Sigma symbols, a mark he had started during spring break, unbeknownst to his family.

But his fraternity brothers took it upon themselves to continue the branding -- this time large triangles to represent the Tri Delta Sorority -- on his other buttock while he was passed out.

Johnson said the Tri Delta mark was mingled with numerous other brands, most of which are unrecognizable, since they overlap.

"They are large," she said.

"I woke up the next morning and I was in a lot of pain," Carter told the Fort Worth Star-Telegram. "My whole other butt cheek was destroyed."

The father of one of the students named by Craven as a possible brander told ABCNews.com that "the way I understand it, [Carter] consented to it."

Johnson said Chance Carter also had defense burns on his hands. The family is unsure if any other students were branded that night. The other fraternity brothers are not speaking to him.

"He's trying to get his life back and unfortunately, that's going to take some time," Johnson said.
Branding has been a rite of passage in black fraternities for decades, but is still a fairly uncommon ritual among white fraternity members.

Lawrence Ross Jr., author of "The Divine Nine: The History of African American Fraternities and Sororities," told ABCNews.com that he's starting to hear more and more cases of branding among white fraternities, which he attributed to Internet videos and pictures glorifying the ritual.
"I tend to look at it as a personal choice," Ross said, adding that he chose a tattoo, not a brand, during his frat days with Alpha Phi Alpha.

A spokeswoman for Texas Christian University issued a statement that school officials were investigating the family's claims.

"TCU began an investigation after the family informed us of this incident. University policy prohibits harming another student, which would obviously include branding," the statement read. "It's too early to tell if this incident was related to a student-sponsored activity, but the health and safety of our students is of utmost importance to TCU."

. . .

12   Netter Sarah.. "Texas Fraternity Brother Branded, Family Furious Over Ritual" ABC World News. 29 January 2010.

CASE HISTORY 6 13
Boulder, CO

What began as a dream pledge party turned into a nightmare for fraternity pledges and for the University of Colorado at Boulder when nine prospective brothers were arrested this weekend after police said they drunkenly ransacked a pair of motel rooms.

The Estes Park Police responded to an anonymous report of a disruption inside a local Super 8 motel room in the early morning hours on Sunday.

Inside the motel rooms, they said they found nine male students from the University of Colorado, according to a press release by Estes Park Police, and more than a $1,000 worth of damage in the two adjoining rooms.

"Several of the freshman fraternity brothers from Delta Chi told officers that they were dropped off ... by older fraternity members and were told to get to know each other," the release stated. To help that happen, they were provided with a keg of beer and several bottles of liquor, police said.

Delta Chi Fraternity Inc., the fraternity's national headquarters based in Iowa City, Iowa, has suspended the Boulder chapter, executive director Ray Galbreth told ABC News. "They are under suspension pending our investigation," Galbreth said.

Police said the fraternity brothers-in-training responded to the get-to-know assignment with reckless zeal, leaving a scene that included one large hole in a wall and several smaller holes scattered around the rooms. Ceiling fans and heating units had been ripped from walls; shower curtains and rods had been torn down; one mirror was covered with wads of spit and another was shattered, according to police, who added that blood and vomit were splattered all over the place.

In all, nine pledges were taken into custody and booked at the Larimer County Detention Center. They are Nicholas Mortimer, William Martin, Andrew Sapiro, Britt Cherster, Kyle Jungels, Anthony Cronin, Matthew Bowen, Lukas Feyh and Kyle Maltz. The group includes freshmen, sophomores and one senior, according to the University of Colorado community directory.

One of the students, William Martin, a freshman political science major, responded to an e-mail sent by ABC News to all nine of the alleged offenders asking if there was another side of the story.

"nobody (sic) ever looks at the good things a person does with their life," Martin wrote, describing a trip to Mexico during which he built houses and other volunteer work feeding the hungry.

86

"But as soon as we make a mistake everyone is incredibly quick to judge us. yes (sic) we made a huge mistake, and I feel absolutely horrible about the situation. but (sic) the only way to live a valid life is to learn from our mistakes so as not to repeat them ever again."

Martin went on to question the validity of the national coverage the story has received.
"everyone (sic) in colorado (sic) already despises us, is it your attempt to have the entire nation despise us?" he wrote. "we are intelligent, bright, and caring people who made an extremely stupid, unintelligent, and disrespectful mistake that doesn't reflect who we are, but that doesn't seem to matter to anybody."

Bronson Hilliard, a spokesman for the University of Colorado, said as the students make their way through the county judicial system they could face unspecified punishment from the university. The campus burden of proof in those cases can be less than in the courts, Hilliard told ABC News. 12

. . .

13 Schoetz David. " Frat's Motel Pledge Event Turns Berserk "
ABC WORLD NEWS.. 20 Feb , 2008

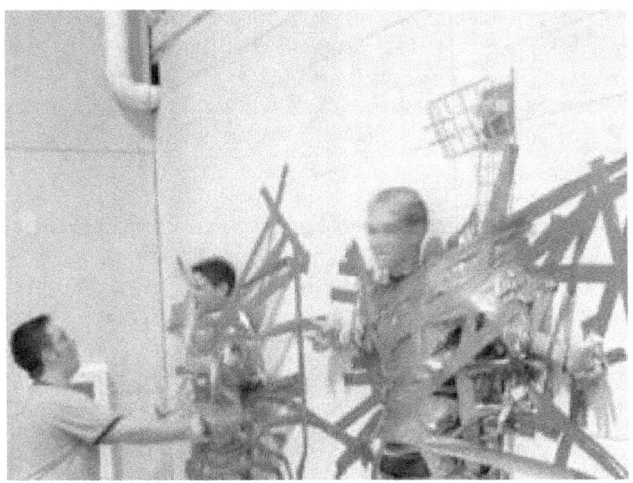

The heartbroken mother of a Cornell University sophomore is suing a fraternity for $25 million after members allegedly kidnapped her son, blindfolded him, bound his hands and feet, and forced him to drink so much alcohol that he passed out and died.

George Desdunes, the son of a Haitian immigrant, was pronounced dead on Feb. 25 from alcohol poisoning at Cayuga Medical Center. Desdunes' blood alcohol level was .409 – more than five times the legal limit, according to the family's lawsuit.

Desdunes' mother, Marie Lourdes Andre, is suing Sigma Alpha Epsilon fraternity for $25 million in the wrongful death of her only son.

The aspiring doctor was captured by freshmen "pledges" of the fraternity who allegedly devised a horrific set of tasks and punishments for Desdunes and one other frat member.

"I call it inmates running the institution," said Andre's lawyer, William Friedlander, referring to the SAE hazing. "This is a terrible tragic case. He was a really great kid."

Desdunes, 19, a member of the SAE fraternity, was grabbed by the freshmen pledges who tied him up with zip ties and duct tape.

The pledges are alleged to have asked him trivia questions about the fraternity. If he answered incorrectly he reportedly had to do exercises such as sit-ups, or consume various foods and drinks including sugar, flavored syrups and vodka.

Desdunes reportedly passed out, but instead of being brought to a hospital he was allegedly taken to the fraternity house while still bound, and left on a couch in the library.

A housekeeper discovered Desdunes and called 911, and Desdunes was later pronounced dead at Cayuga Medical Center.

Another SAE member, Gregory Wyler, had been kidnapped the same night, and Desdunes' roommate had locked their bedroom door to avoid his own kidnapping.

Andre said in her lawsuit that her son hoped to be a doctor, and was a former altar boy who played varsity soccer and the trumpet.

She said in a statement, "With the death of my son, I find some comfort in knowing that this lawsuit may bring about changes in fraternities that will prevent other families from suffering as I have."

In the past year Friedlander and his co-counsel have prosecuted more than 15 hazing cases and most of them, he said, involved deaths from drinking.

Friedlander said at least five other deaths have occurred at SAE chapters since 1997.

SAE has more than 240 chapters and nearly 300,000 initiates.

The fraternity released a statement in response to the lawsuit, referencing SAE's "zero-tolerance policy" for members who don't comply with regulations: "Members are expected to adhere to our fraternity policies and to uphold behavior consistent with our creed, 'The True Gentleman.'"

SAE also made note that it sponsors an anonymous hazing hotline at 1-888-NOT-HAZE.

"There's absolutely nothing this organization endorses or publishes that would be an endorsement for hazing," Sigma Alpha Epsilon spokesman Brandon Weghorst told ABCNews.com. "Our leadership won't hesitate to take action against individuals who do not follow our regulations or who breech our risk management."

In response to Desdunes' death, Cornell withdrew recognition of SAE for the next five years which means the fraternity will not operate on Cornell's campus during that time.

In a statement Cornell University spokesman Tommy Bruce said the school would be following the litigation closely, and "Cornell University neither condones nor tolerates hazing or the type of activities that we understand contributed to George's death."

. . .

14 CHRISTINA CARON ABC NEWS "Cornell University Frat House Sued for $25 Million Over House Hazing Death" 28 June 2011.

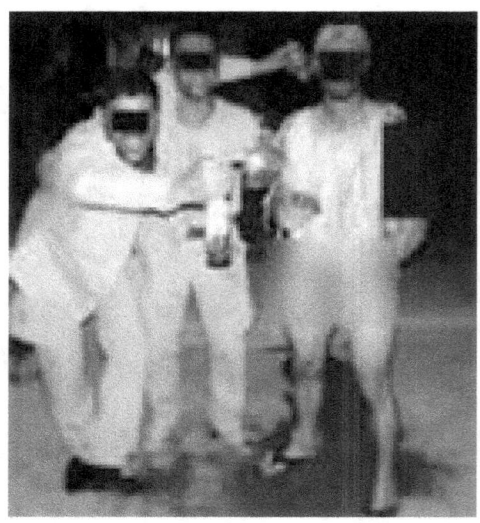

SAN MARCOS, Texas -- A fraternity hazing incident has landed 20 Texas State University students in jail.

Hazing is illegal at Texas State University, but students will tell you it's still a common recruiting practice in the Greek system.

"Strapped down to chairs, being forced to chug large amounts of alcohol," said student Robby Rumley.

Members of the Sigma Nu fraternity are facing accusations of doing something similar.

University police say on Sept. 12, 10 Sigma Nus with the help of 10 female students, picked up students wishing to join the fraternity from their homes. Police say the pledges were blindfolded and told to strip down to their underwear.

They were driven to the Bishop Square Apartments, Northwest of campus. Police say they were led inside an apartment garage, still blindfolded, and were seated on the floor. Police say they were provided with alcohol and told they had to drink in order to get into the fraternity.

In the weeks following, police arrested the 20 students and charged them with hazing or failing to report it. Each charge carries a fine up to $2,000 and a sentence of up to six months in jail.

This is the second time in recent years that Sigma Nu has been in trouble with the law. In 2003, the university suspended the chapter for two years following a party where fraternity members served alcohol to minors. The president and vice president of the fraternity were arrested for the alcohol charge. Two other members were arrested for assault on a police officer and evading arrest.

A spokesperson at Sigma Nu headquarters in Virginia released a statement to KVUE about the recent accusations.

"The chapter is fully cooperating with police," said Fred Dobry, director of risk reduction. "We take any allegations related to misconduct seriously and we're to investigate concerns fully with university officials and chapter leadership.

. . .

14 NOELLE NEWTON. "Hazing incident leads to arrest of 20 Texas State students" KVUE News 13 October 2011.

Nearly two dozen fraternity members at Northern Illinois University have been charged with hazing-related counts after a freshman was found dead at their fraternity house following a night of drinking.

DeKalb police and prosecutors issued arrest warrants Monday for 22 members of the Pi Kappa Alpha fraternity in DeKalb. Five members are charged with felony hazing, while the other 17 members are facing misdemeanor hazing charges.

Phone messages and emails sent to local and national fraternity officials were not immediately returned.

The warrants were filed after David Bogenberger, 19, was found unresponsive at the fraternity house early on Nov. 2. The DeKalb County Coroner's Office said toxicology results found his blood alcohol content was about five times the legal limit for driving.

The coroner ruled Bogenberger's cause of death was cardiac arrhythmia, with alcohol intoxication as a contributing cause.

The DeKalb Police Department said its investigation found the fraternity hosted an unsanctioned event on Nov. 1 that wasn't registered with the university or the fraternity's national chapter.

"The event that night involved the pledges rotating between several rooms in the fraternity house, being asked a series of questions, and then being provided cups of vodka and other liquor to drink," police said in a statement. "This resulted in the pledges drinking a large quantity of alcohol in about a two-hour time period."

Police said several other pledges reported getting sick and passing out due to excessive alcohol consumption.

In addition to the charges, NIU said 31 students are accused of violating the school's code of conduct. Those students could face penalties ranging from reprimand to expulsion.

Bogenberger's family said in a statement that they appreciate law enforcement professionals who investigated his death and "seek accountability for a horrible event."

"We have no desire for revenge," the family said. "Rather, we hope that some significant change will come from David's death. Alcohol poisoning claims far too many young, healthy lives.

"We must realize that young people can and do die in hazing rituals. Alcohol-involved hazing and initiation must end."

. . .

^ *NIU frat members charged in student hazing death* Peoria Journal Star. 18 December 2012

In the fore mentioned case, on February 15, 2013, the fraternity quickly found itself in costly litigation as reported by the regional newspaper, the Peoria Journal Star, over the hazing:

DEKALB —

The family of a Northern Illinois University freshman who died after a night of heavy drinking has filed a wrongful death lawsuit against the fraternity he was pledging.

Nineteen-year-old David Bogenberger was found dead at Pi Kappa Alpha fraternity on Nov. 2.

94

The night before, he and other pledges had attended an event there that the national fraternity organization says it did not sanction.

Toxicology results found Bogenberger's blood alcohol content was about five times the legal limit for driving.

The family's lawsuit says members of the fraternity failed to seek medical attention after the pledge had become unconscious.

Five fraternity members have been charged with felony hazing. Seventeen others face misdemeanor hazing charges.

The fraternity's national office in Memphis did not immediately return a call seeking comment Friday.

CASE HISTORY 9 15
Sorority Hazing Increasingly Violent, Disturbing

Joanne said she had to stand silently with her nose touching a cold, dirty wall while her potential sorority sisters screamed that she wasn't worth their time. If the pledges moved at all, Joanne said, one of the four Penn State Altoona sorority members would shove their heads into the concrete bricks until they had lumps or bruises.

Even now, Joanne said, a year later, she still gets harassed by her former sorority sisters, which is why she asked that her real name not be used. When she first decided to pledge as freshman, and eventually join, a sorority at Penn State-Altoona, Joanne had hoped for the comfortable camaraderie of a close-knit group of friends; not "the semester from hell."

"One night the sisters made us cook them dinner," she said. "Since I obviously wasn't into cooking and then cleaning their dishes, the sisters forced me to clean the kitchen floor. I didn't have any gloves and they would tell me to do it again until it was spotless. I used my fingernails to scrub the ground.

"The water was pitch black," Joanne continued. "They asked me to drink it. I refused and left the apartment. I ended up coming back [to carry out a different punishment] because they called me and yelled at me. I didn't know what else to do."

Experts say hazing has grown increasingly violent among sororities.

Joanne's experience in the fall of 2008 is one example of an ingrained cultural tradition called hazing, which, experts say, has triggered increasing violence among women that can lead to depression and self-esteem problems as the hazers take cues from reality TV or try to emulate the behavior of male fraternities.

Other examples range from simple name-calling to the demeaning practice of "boob ranking."

Elizabeth Allan and Mary Madden of the University of Maine-Orono point to their research as evidence of its pervasiveness, even though most colleges have policies banning the practice.

"We found that 68 percent of women in Greek life have experienced hazing in order to become a member of these groups," Allan said, based on the 2007 findings in their National Study of Student Hazing, which tabulated e-mail questionnaire responses from more than 11,000 students at 53 different institutions.

Joanne has plenty of experience.

She said the Penn State-Altoona pledges would get calls at 2 a.m. demanding that they gather for a meeting at the sorority president's apartment as soon as possible.

"They would test us on one of the sorority's prayers or songs, and if we got it wrong they would call us fat or ugly until we cried," Joanne said. "So many of us cried in front of them."

After Joanne got fed up with the hazing, she sent an e-mail to Tracy Maxwell, the executive director of Hazing Prevention, one of the leading non-profit organizations working to eradicate hazing. Eventually, the sorority's national organization began to investigate the sorority chapter.

An executive at the sorority confirmed that the national office investigated the hazing claims and took disciplinary actions. The sorority would not disclose its findings.

Marissa Carney, a spokesperson for Penn State Altoona, said the school was not notified of Joanne's allegations. In an e-mail to ABC News L. Jay Burlingame, the Director of the Office of Judicial Affairs at Penn State Altoona, said that the school takes accusations of hazing in its sororities and fraternities seriously, and that these allegations are "immediately referred to and investigated by the appropriate college office."

Burlingame added, "Penn State Altoona strictly prohibits any and all activities, actions, or situations which recklessly or intentionally endanger the mental or physical health or safety of a student."

Joanne said she switched campuses at the end of her first year because of the hazing. But despite the switch, Joanne said, she is still receiving hateful Facebook posts and messages from the young women she once called sisters.

"All the sisters and pledges turned on me," Joanne said. "My car was keyed. I was getting threatening text messages every day. The second semester I couldn't sleep because I would have nightmares."

Dan McCarthy, who runs the Hazing Hotline for the law firm Manley Burke in Cincinnati, said the hotline received 55 calls from mid-August to mid-December in 2009, its third year in business.

"Last year, for the entire year, we received 150 calls and we expect to receive around the same amount this year," McCarthy said, adding that the calls were split between the genders.

'Pure Emotional Blackmail'

Sally Spencer-Thomas, a suicide expert and author of "Violence Goes to College," said she was hazed while joining a co-ed fraternity in the late 1980s. Spencer-Thomas defines hazing as "the pure, emotional blackmail of a person.

"Students join these organizations because they want a quick group of friends," Spencer-Thomas said. "Even though the pledges form close bonds from surviving the hazing together, they often have invisible scars."

Invisible scars can mean anything from depression to a lack of self-esteem resulting from the hazing. But the scars can also be visible.

CASE HISTORY 10
Cover Ups and Conspiracies

Tyler Kinglade, write for the Huffington Post reported on the hazing death in December 2013 and subsequent attempted cover-up by a fraternity at Baruch College. His article reports that. "Police say members of Pi Delta Psi at Baruch College tried to cover up the fraternity hazing that caused the death of 19-year-old Chun "Michael" Deng.

Deng, 19, died as a result of injuries sustained during a hazing activity called "The Gauntlet" and the "Glass Ceiling" by various news outlets. Pledges like Deng were blindfolded and forced to carry backpack filled with 20 pounds of sand, the Pocono Record reports. Brothers then took turns trying to knock the pledges down. Deng was knocked to the ground and injured his head, police said, which ultimately led to the brain trauma that killed him.

The incident took place at a residence at the Poconos in Pennsylvania on Dec. 8. Deng was pronounced dead on Dec. 9. Baruch is part of the City University of New York system.

Police said the fraternity brothers did not call 911, and took more than 90 minutes to seek medical attention for Deng. In the mean time, before deciding to drive him to the hospital, the brothers searched for information online about Deng's symptoms.

The young men who brought Deng to the hospital at first said they were wrestling when he hit his head, according to WNBC.

Students also tried to cover up their fraternity ties. NBC News reports Deng's big pledge brother, Charles Lai, called the house in the Poconos from the hospital and told them to hide anything fraternity-related.

Deng had no alcohol or drugs in his system, but the New York Daily News reports that police did find magic mushrooms and marijuana in a vehicle belonging to the fraternity brothers".

The Trend Toward Violence

A Sigma Gamma Rho pledge at Rutgers University in New Brunswick, N.J., went to the hospital last month because of injuries allegedly sustained during a violent paddling incident.

The school arrested six girls from the sorority the night the pledge went to the hospital. All six girls have since been released on bail and have entered not guilty pleas. Gregory Blimling, the university's vice president of student affairs, said, "When we hear about [hazing] issues, we move aggressively to stop them.

"Rutgers has a no tolerance policy. Every student organization is required to go through an anti-hazing workshop and sign a pledge saying they will not participate in hazing."

Despite that, a 21-year-old senior at Rutgers University who said she is friends with the sorority members who allegedly paddled the pledge said that hazing in campus sororities was common.

"Hazing is something that everyone knows is going on here on campus," the senior said, requesting anonymity. "All the fraternities and sororities use paddles here. It is really nothing new at all.

"People are just more upset that this girl ratted. Some people actually found out who the girl that ratted is and she will probably be shunned now. They probably won't, like, talk to her at Greek events or anything."

Maxwell of Hazing Prevention said that violent hazing seems to have worsened in the past five to 10 years.

"Hazing is a societal problem," she said. "Especially with reality-TV shows forcing people to do something crazy to win a prize. I am sensing some of the hazing happening today is for entertainment purposes. Now we are seeing more of a prevalence of hazing based around, 'Let's see what we can get them to do.'"

Maxwell said she often receives e-mails from distressed girls like Joanne who say they have nowhere else to turn.

"I received an e-mail last week in which a girl told me that her sisters said she had to either take a hit of cocaine or use a dildo in front of them," Maxwell said. "Another woman from New York sent me a detailed schedule of the hazing that she was subjected to, and the sheer hours involved were more than a full-time job. The sessions went all night in some cases and were often violent."

Rhea Almeida, founder of the Institute for Family Studies in New Jersey and board member of the Council on Contemporary Families, said one reason violence and male-oriented hazing activities are becoming more commonplace among females could be because "in opposing femininity, girls feel popular and strong.

"Today, women are experiencing different gender roles and therefore are using more aggression and violence than they did a decade ago," Almeida said.

The University of Maine's Allan echoed that sentiment in a chapter she wrote for "The Hazing Reader" by Hank Nuwer, titled "Hazing and Gender: Analyzing the Obvious." Allan wrote, "Increasingly, girls and women gain credibility and status by proving they are tough, rugged and strong."

Alexandra Robbins, author of the book "Pledged: The Secret Life of Sororities," said, "I saw a definite trend toward physical methods."

Robbins spent a year undercover following four sorority girls and was surprised by the amount of physical hazing that the women experienced, she said.

"One example was a girl named Arika whose pledge class had to answer trivia questions and drink straight vodka when they got a question wrong," Robbins said. "They were also presented with a sharpie, a knife, a hammer and a dildo and the sisters said if they got enough wrong they would be violated with one of those four.

"Arika ended up walking out but then she decided to stay in the sorority because her whole family had gone Greek and they said that's just what happens. That's how ingrained hazing is."

Emotional Hazing: Just as Harmful

Even though there is a growing trend toward violence in sororities, the emotional hazing that women's organizations have long been known for is still pervasive and equally scarring.

Emotional hazing can be hard to define but experts say it can include verbal harassment, such as calling a pledge fat or ugly, and games or rituals that aren't physically abusive but can leave an emotional mark: yelling out how much someone weighs or circling the fat on their bodies.

Some national organizations even define it as anything that differentiates pledges from sisters, meaning it can include sorority members telling pledges when to go out, who to speak to or what to wear.

The Cornell University chapter of the Pi Beta Phi sorority sent a seven-page e-mail to its pledges in January detailing what is and isn't appropriate to wear at different functions. The tone of the e-mail -- with lines such as "No muffin tops or camel toe" and "I will not tolerate any gross plastic shizz [jewelry]" -- drew criticism from the Huffington Post and many online young adult forums.

The Pi Beta Phi national headquarters does not believe that the e-mail constitutes hazing but, according to a statement e-mailed to ABC News from their Executive Director Juli Willeman, "The content in this communication in no way reflects the values of Pi Beta Phi nor the policy the sorority follows in its recruitment of new members."
Hazing Prevention's Maxwell, as with many other experts, said that psychological and emotional hazing is anything that will damage someone's self-esteem.

"This type of hazing takes a group of individuals who already have issues with self-worth and highlights them," Maxwell said.

"You never know what kind of psychological trauma a girl may have in their background or what kind of mental health issues they may have."

Lining Up in Order of Breast Size

Robbins ran into a lot of emotional hazing while researching her book, calling "boob ranking" one of the worst.

"The sisters would bring pledges into a cold room and tell them to strip off their shirts and bras and line-up in order of breast size," Robbins said. "Then they played mental games with the girls and made fun of them.

"Another woman I spoke with was forced to stand on a bench in front of a fraternity and everybody got to yell out parts of her body that need work. This happened in the '90s and almost a decade later she still had emotional scars."

Mike Dilbeck, the president of Beck and Co., a nonprofit video production service, and the creator and producer of the RESPONSE ABILITY Project, an educational video program that addresses bystander behavior, used to be the president of a fraternity, which was kicked off campus for hazing, among other reasons, years after he graduated.

Dilbeck said that the worst part of emotional hazing is that it could "validate things that women could already be saying to themselves.

"When you're told stuff like you're too fat, you're ugly and you can't dress right, it takes an internal toll on young women," Dilbeck said. "It can have a long-lasting emotional impact on them."

Hank Nuwer, author of four books on hazing, echoed the idea that sisters can forget about the emotional state of their pledges.

"The girls need to remember that you don't know somebody's background during an initiation," Nuwer said. "You are playing with a loaded weapon when you emotionally haze."

Even though there is more awareness of the issue than ever before, it continues to be a major part of today's Greek life.

Robbins said that getting rid of hazing is easy: just get rid of pledging.

"Sororities are just social groups and it is ludicrous and pointless to have pledges 'earn' their letters," Robbins said. "These girls are fresh to college and vulnerable. It is hard to stand up when you have a sorority telling you have to do something or get kicked out."

Many experts believe that students must take it upon themselves to stop hazing.

"It can't be only policy because that just drives hazing underground," Spencer-Thomas said. "It has to be students saying it's time for no more death and no more loss. There are other proven ways to forge bonds than to hurt people."

For Joanne, she said, switching campuses and meeting a new group of friends has given her a renewed sense of confidence.

After the sorority's national organization completed its investigation, two members of the chapter were dismissed from the sorority and two other members were put on probation.

While Joanne said that the girls continue to harass her on Facebook via "mean" postings, she tries to ignore them and to focus on the people in her life that build her up.

"My experience made me scared to think about who I can trust and who I can't," Joanne said. "When I was on the other campus, I never understood why people said college was the best time of your life. This year is a complete 180-degree change and I am really happy."

. . .

15 COURTNEY CROWDER. Sorority Hazing Increasingly Violent, Disturbing. ABC NEWS. 17 Feb 2010.

SIX STEPS FOR PREVENTING HAZING ON YOUR TEAM

Professionals suggest six steps that can and must take to greatly minimize the chances that a hazing incident will occur on your team.

1. Develop Strong, Positive, Responsible Leaders

It always puzzles me when schools are looking for an anti-hazing speaker or program. When it comes right down to it, what these schools really want and need are positive, responsible, and proactive leaders who will not plan or permit any hazing. Invest the time to develop strong leaders who aren't afraid to step up and speak out against hazing.

2. Provide Positive Alternatives to Hazing

Ironically, some team leaders believe that hazing promotes team building, when in actuality it undermines it. If team building is what they are after, then there are a variety of positive team building ideas that leaders can use like team dinners, movie nights, ropes courses, camping trips, whitewater rafting, laser tag, team building challenges, etc. As a coach, you can either organize these team building ideas or empower your team leaders to do so.

3. Meet with Your Leaders and Team to Discuss Your Views and Policy on Hazing

Make sure your leaders and team members know in no uncertain terms that hazing will not be tolerated in your program/school. Let your leaders know that you are holding them accountable to prevent and diffuse any potential hazing incidents BEFORE they happen. Be clear that the consequences for them and the team will be quite severe if they do not heed your warning.

(Remember, if you suspect hazing may occur at a party, yet say nothing, your athletes in effect will likely believe that you condone the behavior.)

4. Cite Examples of Initiations Gone Bad

To help the message sink in to your athletes, you might consider giving your leaders examples of teams that have lost teammates and/or seasons because of hazing incidents. Calling attention to these real-life examples is especially important if you believe your athletes have a careless attitude toward hazing. These terrible, yet practical examples can help them understand the seriousness of the situation.

5. Install a Buddy System

Pair up your newcomers with one of your veteran athletes. Let the veteran know that they are in charge of helping the newcomer survive and thrive in the new environment. You want to create a situation where the older teammate acts as a big brother/sister for the younger one and looks out for him/her. Impress upon the veteran that they must always look out for and protect their younger teammate.

6. Encourage Your Newcomers to Report Any Anticipated or Actual Hazing

Let your newcomers know that you want them to come to you immediately if they anticipate or experience any hazing. Obviously most will be unlikely to do so because they want to fit in to the team and the last thing they want is their teammates to view them as a tattletale. However, be sure that they too know that you have zero tolerance for hazing.

While unfortunately these suggestions can never guarantee that you won't have a hazing incident, proactively using these suggestions provides you with the best insurance policy against it.

MILITARY HAZING

Military Discipline or a Tradition Whose Time Is Past?

Precisely what military hazing is, however, defies definition. One recruit's hazing is another's "shape- up" exercises. Most civilian definitions of hazing fail to take account of its varied meanings in military life. The term "hazing" can be used to describe anything from a good-natured punch on the stripes when someone is promoted, to Navy chiefs who make a new chief wear a dress, to boot camp activities when superiors or peers try to transform a balky recruit into a trustworthy team player. There also are degrees of hazing, and in any of the above examples one could find people crossing lines that shouldn't be crossed.

Of course, hazing is not exclusive to the U.S. military. Hazing is widespread in the Canadian, Czech and Russian armed forces. In Russia, many first-year soldiers die at the hands of their superiors whom they call "grandfathers." Others endure sadistic demands such as licking a toilet bowl clean, says Charles Moskos, a Northwestern University sociology professor and chairman of the Inter-University Seminar on Armed Forces and Society. There's a Difference. Hazing in the United States goes beyond the military.

High school upperclassmen, bands, professional athletic teams and adult and collegiate secret-letter societies haze. Today, mainly because of fraternity hazing deaths,39 states forbid hazing. Significantly, most experts distinguish military hazing from fraternity hazing. The purpose and result of military hazing - keeping troops alive - doesn't apply to Greeks bearing paddles. Although the first scandals involving hazing in U.S. service academies began over a century ago, the general public heard little about hazing in the military branches until 1956. That year all training procedures went under a microscope following the drowning deaths of recruit sat Parris Island. Demands that military hazing stop escalated in the late 1960s after one national magazine exposed unusually vigorous artillery OCS hazing conducted by Vietnam returnees. Today, stories about hazing in the military are commonplace. Three Marines were charged with miscellaneous offenses in 1999 in Okinawa, Japan, after an initiation allegedly injured the hand of a Marine. A 1998 scandal occurred at Fort Knox, Ky., after a Marine's classmates beat him during a ritual-like "love session." Video recordings of Marines involved in so-called blood pinnings filled the airwaves a few years ago.

Consequently, dozens of hazers were disciplined in military justice courts during the 1990s for miscellaneous offenses. Julian Neiser, a former drill instructor, worked at Parris Island and saw the careers of honorable men self-destruct. "I've seen guys who were excellent Marines, combat veterans, guys who were extremely qualified, do something stupid to a recruit," says Neiser. "Before they knew it, their careers were ruined. They were wearing orange jumpsuits and picking up trash on sides of the roads." Hazing Headlines. What's responsible for

110

today's hazing furor? Joe Jansen, a former Marine sergeant, points to instantaneous communication on the Internet and on CNN. In particular, witnesses to hazings use video cameras to capture secret rituals on tape and give or sell them to media producers who can count on a quick ratings shot in the arm, he says. The result is public outrage. "I don't think society has a natural aversion to rites of passage and ritual," says Jansen. "But I think society does have an aversion to senseless brutality." Ironically, some hazing activities continue in spite of American press opposition. Richard Sigal, a New Jersey sociologist who writes about hazing, says press scrutiny fails to check all but the most severe hazing, driving it underground and causing officials to give lip service to eliminating it. Shared Misery. Experts suspect it's not the actual hazing that super-glues young recruits together but the sharing of experiences that try their souls and give a feeling of satisfaction if endured. "Going through shared misery is what bonds people, not hazing per se," Moskos says. After lights go out during basic, jokesters usually start a running banter. They good-naturedly make fun of the system and their drill sergeants who tell them they are tearing them down to put them back together.

Recruits who were humiliated that day can re-invent their experiences in a humorous light by seeing how things looked through the eyes of their fellow soldiers. Often they laugh until the tears come, says Moskos, then hop to their tasks the next morning with new resolve. Rite of Passage. Maj. John Jansen, a Marine stationed in California, says a matter of degree separates activities that constitute an acceptable military rite of passage and unacceptable behavior that rightfully gets perpetrators in trouble with the Uniform Code of Military Justice. For Jansen, a non-objectionable and perhaps necessary rite of passage would be a symbolic gesture to acknowledge a troop's new rank, so long as that might involve nothing more than a non-hurtful, symbolic blow. For example: When a lance corporal becomes a corporal and NCO, his peers and sometimes superiors will punch him on there "blood" stripe

111

outside his dress blues trousers. No nudity is involved nor any suffering more than momentary stinging pain.

In contrast, Jansen sees no justification in the Marine paratrooper blood pinnings that have been shown in gruesome detail on television and Internet news programs. In various videotapes that surfaced between 1991 and 1997, Marines were shown ramming symbolic gold-wing pins into the chests of those who had fulfilled a 10-jump requirement. "That was so wrong it wasn't funny," says Jansen. "The guys looked like captives, screaming, yelling and gnashing their teeth. This kind of hazing, no question, is wrong and the Marine Corps doesn't countenance that kind of behavior."

Studies Needed. Consider military rites of passage that cause neither injuries nor lasting pain, and aren't taken to dangerous extremes by sadists or negligent individuals. At least one expert thinks they should be tolerated within reason, seeing value over a long period of time in the tribal initiations that signify and shape a child's entrance into adulthood. "You can't have a rite of passage without some hazing," says Moskos, who vigorously condemns hazing taken to an extreme. "A zero tolerance for hazing is counterproductive." Studies in sociology and psychology are still academic infants compared to some other disciplines. No reputable scholar has spent time fully studying the pro-and-con effects of rites of passage in a military setting, although several have written about pollywog ceremonies for scholarly journals interested in folklore.

Studies into behavior during initiations that have been done are old and in need of reassessment. An oft-cited 1958 study, financed by the National Science Foundation, tried to assess the effect of severity of initiation on personal preference for a group. The research, performed by Elliot Aronson and Judson Mills determined that a severe initiation did make individuals like a group more. Certainly Tom Hohan, now a New Orleans businessman, outright rejects that the intense physical hazing he endured to complete OCS training in the late1960s made him like his artillery outfit more.

"I hated it," he says.

Nor did he bond with his fellow recruits, all of whom were competing with him for officer slots. "Out of the 74 or 76 who graduated, I'd be surprised if 10 percent would differ from me about hating it." POW Camp. Drafted out of a Pennsylvania steel mill in1968, Hohan joined 140 other males in artillery Officer Candidate School at Ft. Sill, Okla.A mere 40 percent graduated, including Hohan, one of only two non-college men to do so. Hazing - or a combination of hazing and discipline building - claimed the rest, says Hohan, who since has become a University of South Carolina graduate. "Hazing during OCS was legendary and the POW camp you had to experience, if caught during an escape-and-evasion exercise, was pure hell."

Hohan has vivid recollections of the two years, 10 months and three days he spent in the military. He recalls saluting a goldfish and waiting for it to swim around and face him before he was allowed to shower. Mostly he recalls a torturous prisoner-of-war simulation that seemed more real to him than an actual exercise. Hardened veterans back from Vietnam had the OCS candidates lift telephone poles, endure long periods in stocks and maneuver through mud laced with traces of fecal material. All that would make Hohan a firm opponent of hazing - right?

Wrong.

"It helped me survive," says Hohan, who says the hazing gave him the mental toughness to survive in Vietnam and to survive punishing deadlines in the real world after his mustering out. Neiser, now working in Pittsburgh and attending law school, agrees with that assessment. He cautions that turning out sloppy soldiers who can't be counted on in wartime is no solution to the hazing problem. Every day, as Neiser exited through the rear hatch o fthe school at Parris Island he reread a sign that bore into his very core. "Let no man's ghost say, 'If only your training program had done its

113

job.'"

. . .

16 Hank Nuwer *Hazing: Separating Rites From Wrongs*American Legion Magazine, July Issue, Vol. 147, No. 1

CASE HISTORY 1 17
ARMY

Under Army rules, a superior is allowed to subject a soldier to certain kinds of "corrective measures," including "verbal reprimands and a reasonable number of repetitions of authorized physical exercises."

But in light of charges filed this week against eight soldiers in connection with the death of Pvt. Danny Chen, a fellow soldier in Afghanistan, the line separating acceptable activities from hazing, which is forbidden, has come under renewed scrutiny both inside and outside the military.

"It's important to know that Army training is rigorous and demanding and it's often associated with violent action, but we're very careful and very attentive to crossing that line," George Wright, an Army spokesman at the Pentagon, said Thursday. "While we want to make our soldiers tough and resilient, we want to make sure that our training is not abusive."

To that end, officials explained, all officers, both commissioned and noncommissioned, are trained in the distinctions during basic training and during refresher courses throughout their careers.

On Thursday, Gen. Martin E. Dempsey, chairman of the Joint Chiefs of Staff, said on his Facebook page that military officials were investigating several other allegations of hazing. "These appear to be isolated instances of misconduct," he said. "We are duty bound to protect one another from hazing in any form."

Private Chen's body was found on Oct. 3 in a guard tower on his base in southern Afghanistan. He had suffered what the military called "an apparent self-inflicted gunshot wound." The eight service members — one officer and seven enlisted soldiers — were charged with a range of crimes, including manslaughter and negligent homicide, officials announced on Wednesday.

One suspect, Specialist Ryan J. Offutt, 32, of Greenville, Pa., was sentenced to jail in 2002 after pleading guilty to charges of simple assault and indecent assault after attacking a woman in his house in 2001, according to court records and a 2002 account in a local newspaper.

In the Chen case, Specialist Offutt was charged with multiple counts, including involuntary manslaughter, assault consummated by battery, negligent homicide and reckless endangerment.

The authorities have revealed little about the circumstances surrounding the death, which remains under investigation. But Private Chen's parents insisted that their son displayed no suicidal or depressive tendencies. They said Army officials had told them that in the hours before his death, Private Chen was harassed by fellow soldiers, who dragged him out of bed, pelted him with rocks and made him do painful exercises when he failed to turn off a water heater after showering.

According to the family, the soldiers used ethnic slurs against Private Chen, which are also prohibited by Army rules.

Private Chen's parents, Su Zhen Chen and Yan Tao Chen, Chinese immigrants who live in the East Village, said they did not know if their son had done anything else that the other soldiers might have taken as a provocation. But in October, military officials gave the Chens a photocopy of a page from Private Chen's personal journal that included a list, apparently in his handwriting, describing procedural failures: "Didn't clear weapon," "Didn't hydrate," and "No attention to detail (little things)."

Army rules define hazing as conduct whereby a service member causes another service member "to suffer or be exposed to an activity that is cruel, abusive, oppressive or harmful."

Advocates for the family, while pressing for a full investigation, have also been lobbying the Army to crack down on hazing and to improve conditions for minorities, particularly soldiers of Asian descent, who enlist at lower rates than other minorities. Military officials said members of the Army — soldiers and civilian employees alike — undergo "equal-opportunity training" annually.

. . .

116

17 KIRK SEMPLE *"After Charging 8, Army Is Scrutinized on Hazing"* NY TIMES.com 22 December , 2011

CASE HISTORY 2
NAVY [18]

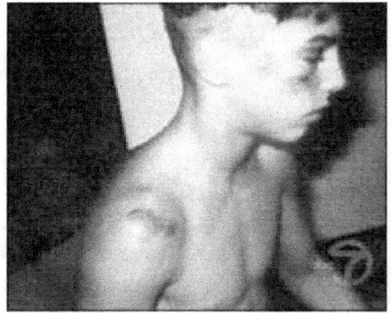

The Navy on Friday said it had fired the commanding officer of a San Diego-based schoolhouse after a hazing investigation.

Capt. Antonio Cardoso, head of Training Support Center San Diego, was fired by Rear Adm. Don Quinn, commander of Naval Education and Training Command, "due to a loss of confidence in Cardoso's ability to command," according to a news release.

Cardoso is the 18th commanding officer fired this year.

Cardoso was fired amid claims of hazing during the course of a captain's mast, the Navy said.

"The investigation centered on personnel ... being required to wear seabags on their backs for extended periods of time," the release said. "The actions were investigated and confirmed as violations of the Navy's policy on hazing."

NETC spokeswoman Cmdr. Kelly Brannon said Marines were made to stand with loaded sea bags while waiting for non-judicial punishment. She wouldn't say how many Marines were involved.

Cardoso, a limited duty officer who took command of TSC San Diego in February 2011, was promoted to captain in 2009, according to Navy Times reports. He has been reassigned to administrative duties at Navy Region Southwest headquarters. Cmdr. Jon Grant, a former executive officer of TSC San Diego, has taken interim command until a permanent relief is chosen.

. . .

17 Sam Fellman Training center CO fired after hazing probe21 September 2012

CASE HISTORY 3
Navy: NORFOLK, VA 18

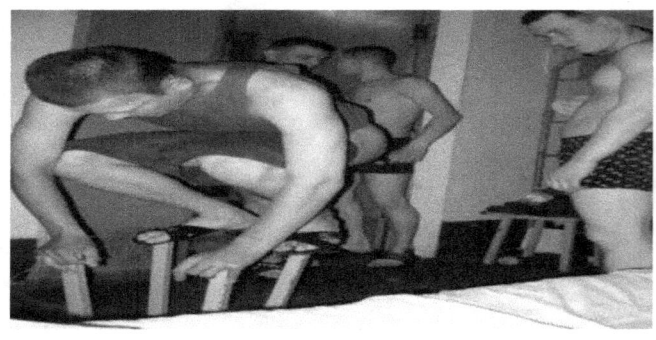

A Navy hazing case that led to the firing of the top enlisted officer aboard a nuclear submarine was sparked by gay jokes about a sailor who said another man tried to rape him while in a foreign port, according to an investigative report obtained by The Associated Press.

The report sheds light on a hazing case that led to the reassignment of Master Chief Machinist's Mate Charles Berry, who had been serving as "chief of the boat" on the Kings Bay, Ga.-based USS Florida.

The Navy announced March 30 that Capt. Stephen Gillespie had relieved Berry as chief, due to dereliction of duty. Aboard a submarine, the chief of the boat advises the commanding officer of issues involving enlisted sailors.

The Navy's announcement said the case involved allegations of hazing aboard Florida, but gave no details. It said Berry was not involved in the hazing, but had knowledge of it and failed to inform his chain of command.

Lt. Brian Wierzbicki, spokesman for Kings Bay's submarine force, said Saturday he did not immediately have a contact number for Berry. The AP left a voice mail message at a phone listed for a Charles Berry in St. Marys, Ga.

An investigative report obtained by The Associated Press under the Freedom of Information Act says the hazing was directed at a sailor who had reported that another man pulled a knife and tried to rape him while in the port at Diego Garcia in the Indian Ocean.

All names in the documents provided to The Associated Press were redacted.

120

The report says the sailor was generally well-liked on the ship and endured the torment for months because he thought it would eventually stop. Among other things, he was called a derogatory term for a gay person and referred to as "Brokeback," a reference to the gay-themed movie "Brokeback Mountain." In addition, someone posted a drawing of a stick figure being sexually assaulted.

Before a group training session on the repeal of the military's "Don't Ask, Don't Tell" policy, the sailor was subjected to comments about coming out of the closet and asked when other sailors could meet his boyfriend and whether his boyfriend was Filipino, the nationality of the person he said tried to rape him.

The report says the sailors who made the derogatory comments didn't realize their shipmate had a knife pulled on him or the psychological toll the comments were taking on him. After eight months of harassment in 2011, the sailor eventually wrote a note saying he had suicidal thoughts and that he could snap and hurt himself or someone else.

The report says there was a culture of hazing and sexual harassment aboard the submarine and there was inadequate knowledge about the Navy's policies against it to stop the behavior before the sailor reached that point.

More counseling and training was ordered at all levels to avoid similar problems in the future.

"The Navy's standards for personal behavior are very high and it demands that sailors are treated with the dignity and respect they deserve. When individuals fall short of this standard of professionalism and personal behavior, the Navy will take swift and decisive action to stop undesirable behavior, protect

121

victims and hold accountable those who do not meet its standards," the Navy said in the March 30 statement.

Berry was temporarily assigned to another post in Kings Bay. Several other junior sailors who participated in the harassment also faced disciplinary action, including loss of rank and pay.

Military suicides in response to hazing have recently gotten the attention of Congress. The nephew of Rep. Judy Chu, D-Calif., killed himself after enduring hazing by his fellow Marines in Afghanistan. A congressional hearing on military hazing was held earlier this year, and Chu is pushing a proposal to better track and define hazing in the Uniform Code of Military Justice.

"We're talking about acts that can result in death, but if not death, then clearly trauma. These are folks that can have post-traumatic stress syndrome because of the acts of others," Chu said. "These are peers administering justice to peers. What happened to the hierarchy that is supposed to be occurring in the military?"

The hazing episode is among a series of embarrassing incidents for the Navy's submarine force that were addressed in a blog post this week by Vice Adm. John Richardson focusing on the importance of character.

"A violation by one seems to be a violation against all," wrote Richardson, the Norfolk-based commander of the Navy's submarine force.

The Navy recently started a training course to discuss real-life examples of bad personal decisions that other officers have made in the past.

The Navy also issued new guidelines earlier this month to ensure that future leaders are all held to the same leadership standards, regardless of their command, during job screening.

. . .

18   Associated Press. Submarine hazing centered on homosexuality 23 June2012

CASE HISTORY 4 [19]
Navy

Navy official Charles Berry was removed because of what he did after a sailor reported an attempted rape.

Navy official Charles Berry was removed from his post aboard the U.S.S. Florida because he failed to take action against gay hazing, according to a recently-released military report.

Before being reassigned in the spring, Berry served as Master Chief Machinist's Mate and Chief of Boat aboard the Navy nuclear submarine. Berry was removed from the ship because he failed to take action against the hazing of a sailor, who was harassed after he reported an attempted rape. The sailor reported that a man held him at knifepoint at the port of Diego Garcia in the Indian Ocean. Other sailors on the U.S.S. Florida discovered the incident and hounded the sailor viciously, hurling gay slurs and jokes at him.

"Among other things, he was called a derogatory term for a gay person and referred to as 'Brokeback,'" the Associated Press reports, "a reference to the gay-themed movie *Brokeback Mountain*. In addition, someone posted a drawing of a stick figure being sexually assaulted." The aggrieved sailor also endured taunting when sailors underwent training for the end of "don't ask, don't tell."

According to the report, the U.S.S. Florida has a culture of antigay harassment and hazing. Berry, who wasn't accused of hazing but simply not doing anything about it, was reassigned, while the accused sailors were reprimanded, and counseling and training was ordered for all on the ship.

. . .

19 Neal Broverman *Navy Official Reassigned After He Fails to Deal With Gay Hazing* The Advocate 25 June 2012

Air Force

After being treated to a nice welcome ceremony with their families, new cadets are separated from their families and loaded onto buses which take them to a different part of the compound. Here a few passages about what follows:

Onboard, the basic cadets looked tight and nervous. One of the more senior cadets had gotten on behind them and immediately began barking out commands to quickly find a seat. He leaned over to me at one point and whispered that "it's about to get loud." And then, without warning to the basic cadets, he began screaming out commands, telling them exactly where to hold their hands, not to speak unless spoken to, that they must recite the seven basic--and only--responses to questions they were now allowed and more.

With that, the doors opened, and the veteran cadets screamed some more, now ordering the newbies off the bus at an even higher volume than before.

The freshmen grabbed their gear and hustled off the bus. They ran to where a cluster of blue-uniformed cadets were waiting in front of a large mat emblazoned with footprints for them to stand on.

A fresh veteran cadet stood in front of the group of newbies and shouted out his commands. That they were to keep their feet each at a 22.5 degree angle from their head, meaning that their feet would be open at a 45 degree angle; that their hands should be held, cupped, at their sides, with their thumbs even with the seams of their pants. And then he ordered his cadre of veteran cadets to "correct" any mistakes they saw in how the new cadets were standing.

This, of course, was their excuse to loudly, energetically, and enthusiastically rush around and berate the newcomers. One by one, it seemed, they would be singled out and screamed at for this or that mistake (see video below). I could tell the veteran cadets were enjoying this, finally their opportunity to shift forward their revenge for when this happened to them two years ago.

It went on for a while, and then, finally and mercifully, it stopped, and the new cadets were ordered to grab their gear and head off up a ramp to begin the next rounds of processing. What surprises me most is not that this type of hazing occurs, but that the CNET author (David Terdiman) maintains a tone of such ambivalence throughout this event. He even decides to commemorate the occassion by taking video and a few snapshots.

I know that what happens on move-in day at AFA is not particularly bad, and really shouldn't surprise us given what we know about discipline models at the service academies. However, when I read this, I immediately think of connections between this and hazing within the Greek system.

(Side note: The friend from my high school class who went to AFA is one of the greatest people I've met and I am in no way trying to impugn the Air Force or the military. I'm sure he would never perpetuate any activity about which we as Americans would not be proud.)

The Line-Up

What this article details is extremely similar to one of the most common forms of fraternity hazing: the line-up. Every house does this differently, but it generally involves having the entire new member ("pledge") class line up for review in front of the brotherhood. New members are usually forced to stay in line for a long period of time, while the brotherhood yells at them, asks them questions about the fraternity, and in some documented cases of hazing, hits them or throws things at them.

The line-up has been at the center of some hazing cases at Cornell. Here is part of the Daily Sun's article about a hazing incident which occurred during my freshman year:

The incident, which took place on the evening of Feb. 23, began when the pledges of Lambda Theta Phi organized themselves in what is known as battle position — hugging each other in a line and squatting. Fraternity brothers than charged at the pledges. In his voluntary statement, a Cornell student and Lambda Theta Phi pledge related that he was removed from the group by Eric Perez, a student at LeMoyne College, and smashed into a sheet rock wall which shattered on impact.

There is also a description of a line-up in the 2004 paper Hazed and Confused (.pdf), which fills 71 pages with anecdotes about the process of pledging a fraternity at Cornell:

Once we reached the house we would have to file down to the basement and take our assigned place in one of two nine person wide, parallel lines, hence the name line up. These infamous lines would shrink and be restructured over time to 6 or 7 man lines not because of any ingenuity on the part of the frat brothers, but rather the glaring awkwardness of not accounting for the fact that our lines were becoming riddled with holes from "pansies" de-pledging.

Once a pledge took his place in line he was not aloud to make eye contact or communicate with any one of his pledge brothers. Line ups would not have been complete without a "pledge educator" also known as brother Russell and every four letter word imaginable when behind tightly closed doors. He frequently led line-ups, which meant leading hazing activities and traumatizing pledges for the entertainment of his frat brothers. Typically he would deride one or all of us, humiliating us with physical actions and/or carefully chosen words while a group of ten to twenty brothers sat around the basement with a six pack of beer or a joint, laughing hysterically and often throwing rotten eggs or insults our way to supplement the experience.

We can draw many similarities between Greek and Air Force pledging. The CNET article notes that, "I could tell the veteran cadets were enjoying this, finally their opportunity to shift forward their revenge for when this happened to them two years ago." This cycle of hazing, in which those who are hazed look forward to having the opportunity to do the same to others, is primarily responsible for perpetuating hazing within the Greek system. Having gone through the same thing, oneself, serves to both legitimize and perpetuate hazing rituals in the mind of the offender.

The purpose of any hazing ritual, if we were to interview those who haze, is to train new members into what is expected of them as members of an organization while also bringing the new member class closer together. In the case of the AFA, what better way to bring together a group of cadets from all 50 states than by putting them through a shared experience of misery?

Is Military Hazing Different?

Some would argue that we should have a different standard for the service academies and the armed forces in general. Sun columnist Munier Salem argued last year that we should accept hazing within the ROTC program, but doubts whether such a program is appropriate for Cornell:

Unity of purpose, strict hierarchies, and "team building" via hazing are all necessary for an effective fighting machine. Doubt is the worst enemy of a well run military. If a soldier is encouraged to doubt his commanding officer, the effective fighting force would quickly dissolve. What I am criticizing is the idea that all this belongs on a college campus.

But even thought the hazing outlined in the CNET article isn't particularly bad, it seems like it's just the tip of the iceberg. The Air Force Academy has been at the center of various scandals and allegations involving hazing:

Ten years after Saum's [rape] case began, the academy is deep in a still-unfolding rape scandal. The charges Saum made about Air Force indifference to crimes at its elite training academy have been picked up by senators, congressmen and dozens of current and former female cadets who are calling for accountability and reform at the academy.

The Air Force itself acknowledges problems, saying at least 56 allegations of sexual assault have been made at the academy during the decade since Saum's complaint.

In an interview with Salon magazine, one military historian speculated that some of the hazing and abuse rituals at the service academies are responsible for the military's treatment of prisoners at Abu Ghraib and our use of torture elsewhere. She details one case:

In Colorado Springs, at the Air Force Academy -- and this did reach the light of day and it was discontinued -- one guy would tightly hold an apple in his rear end and another guy had to eat the apple out of his rear end.

In response to some of these issues, the AFA has tried to rebrand itself while eliminating some of the worst hazing (Tom Roeder, "Class of Change," The Gazette (Colo. Springs), May 29, 2007):

After the sexual assault claims, the academy superintendent and commandant of cadets were replaced. New leaders were handed 165 directives -- an "Agenda for Change" -- to improve the school months before the class of '07 arrived.

"We sort of came in as it started," said senior cadet John Davis. "We haven't known anything but change."

The directives killed the "Bring Me Men" sign and replaced it with a list of "core values." Yelling during basic training was banned. Cadets were separated by gender during training. Hazing rites, including the "recognition" tradition that was in essence "hell week" for freshmen, were outlawed.
Note the bolded line, and think back to the CNET article.

More likely, just as hazing has become entrenched within the rituals of many fraternities and sororities at Cornell, so has it become an accepted part of life at the AFA.

How else can we explain this remarkable passage in a Massachusetts paper about a local cadet who entered AFA a couple of years ago? (Staasi Heropoulos, "Longmeadow Grad Heads For Academy," The Republican (Springfield, Mass.), July 11, 2007)

Auerbach's first year at the academy will be difficult. He and other incoming cadets will endure scorn, abuse and ridicule from upperclassmen and women.

From cleaning his room and polishing his shoes to studying and walking across campus, he'll be told what, when and how to do everything. He will be "ripped on and yelled at" for the entire year.

"It's more for discipline. Before you can be a leader you have to be a follower. They just want to make that point," said Auerbach.

"It's definitely going to be tough, but thousands of people have gone through it before me and they will go through it after me. I want to be there. It's not going to be fun but I'll just have to laugh off the hazing."

This is the same attitude that many new members bring to the fraternity pledging process. They know there might be some hazing and some activities they won't enjoy, but they still join the fraternity because they know the organization stands for something more.

Conclusion: A Double Standard

Here is the point I'm trying to make: If what happens on Day One at the Air Force Academy was observed by a Cornell administrator at a fraternity pledging event, the fraternity would face strong sanctions and its student leaders would face an investigation into their entire new member program. The ensuing report describing the violations would have a tone much different from that of the CNET article.

The reason why such hazing is smiled at in Colorado Springs, yet fought in Ithaca, is that there is a double standard at play. Observers see older cadets yelling at younger cadets in broad daylight, and hear stories of sexual abuse and worse things happening behind closed doors, and dismiss it as part of a necessary process to turn young men and women into military officers who embrace the discipline and hierarchy of our armed forces. After all, joining the military was never supposed to be a fun experience.

The same observers might see fraternity pledges walking to class in funny costumes, or running with their pledge class at early hours of the morning. They might also hear of things like line-ups and much worse rituals which occur behind closed doors. These observers are appalled that such things could happen and question the legitimacy of a system which allows these events to occur.

Dangerous and offensive hazing is never acceptable. It is never right to harm someone physically, or discriminate based on race or sexual orientation, or engage in any sort of torture. But some of the things which our society define as hazing can serve acceptable purposes, both for the military and for Greeks. If our society believes that the hazing at AFA is necessary to establish a sense of order and discipline among the cadets, then we should also recognize that a difficult pledge process can serve to bring a pledge class closer together, help them to better know the brotherhood and its history, and provide them with a sense of accomplishment at the end of the process.

One of the most memorable things I've heard from a Cornell administrator was this: "An activity is considered hazing unless the brothers have to do the same thing as the new members." In our quest to eradicate the ugly forms of hazing from the Greek system, we should not get carried away with eliminating difficult parts of the pledge process which serve legitimate purposes. In our society, the fraternity does not carry the same significance, importance, or respect that the Air Force possesses, but this does not mean that a double standard is acceptable for evaluating what happens to new members. Not everything the Air Force does is good, and not everything the fraternity does is bad. To move forward, this must be our starting point
. . .
20 *Hazing: not just for greeks.* 1 July 2009. Bilmes.blogspot.com

Air Force

Twenty-seven Air Force Academy cadets were injured last week after a traditional hazing event left some with concussions, broken collar bones and cuts and bruises.

One cadet suffered a human bite on the arm, according to an email sent to academy staff by Brig. Gen. Dana Born, dean of cadets.

The hazing, known as First Shirt/First Snow, is an unofficial tradition that occurs every year on the first snow. Freshmen cadets try to throw their stripped-down cadet first sergeant in the snow, while the upperclassmen try to defend the sergeant.

Born's email indicated that what was once a fun event has "turned into a brawl" and has become increasingly violent in the past two years.

This year's hazing sent six cadets — those with concussions and broken collar bones — to local emergency rooms and left 21 others with minor injuries, said John Van Winkle, an academy spokesman.

Van Winkle said the "tradition," which has since been condemned by the academy, roughly dates to the 1980s. Many in the academy, including Van Winkle, had not heard of the event until the injuries were reported. However, it is noted on an academy folklore wiki that describes it this way:

"On the night of the first snow of the season, the smacks storm the first sergeant's room, kidnap him, strip him down to his boxers and carry him outside to drag him around in the snow. Much like nuking, the severity of the operation often depends on the standing of the first sergeant in the eyes of the smacks. A well-liked or well-respected cadet first sergeant will normally not get much more than the cermonial (sic) dragging-through-the-snow. A less-liked or less-respected first sergeant may be bound, nuked in addition, or brought to near-hypothermia."

This is not the first time that out-of-control hazing practices at the academy have come to light or been criticized by authorities. In 2006, in the wake of a sex-assault scandal, an old hazing tradition known as recognition was reinstated after a three-year hiatus in a more neutral form as a focus on physcial endurance for freshmen cadets instead of hazing. At the time, Lt. Gen. John Regni, the school's superintendent, said hazing would not be tolerated.

Most of the academy's 4,000 cadets did not participate in the Oct. 25 first snow hazing, Van Winkle said. The academy is launching a safety investigation into the episode, he said, adding that punitive action is not expected.

"We're going to consider this a teachable moment," Van Winkle said. "They are going to learn from that situation."

The commandant of cadets talked to most of the cadet wing on Friday and Saturday after the event, emphasizing that the tradition "needs to stop and will stop," Van Winkle said.

21 RYAN MAYE HANDY   *27 AFA cadets injured in hazing during first snow.* gazette.com November 01, 2012

CASE HISTORY 7
WOG DAY

Of particular note is the naval tradition of Wog Day. These are events for naval individuals who will cross the Equator for the first time. The question is, is this hazing or mere tradition.

The ceremony of Crossing the Line is an initiation rite in the Dutch merchant navy, Royal Navy, U.S. Navy, U.S. Coast Guard, U.S. Marine Corps, and other navies that commemorates a sailor's first crossing of the Equator.[1] The tradition may have originated with ceremonies when passing headlands, and become a "folly" sanctioned as a boost to morale,[2] or have been created as a test for seasoned sailors to ensure their new shipmates were capable of handling long rough times at sea. Sailors who have already crossed the Equator are nicknamed (Trusty) Shellbacks, often referred to as Sons of Neptune; those who have not are nicknamed (Slimy) Pollywogs (in 1832 the nickname griffins was noted [3]).

Equator-crossing ceremonies, typically featuring King Neptune, are also sometimes carried out for passengers' entertainment on civilian ocean liners and cruise ships. They are also performed in the merchant navy and aboard sail training ships.

The two-day event (evening and day) is a ritual in which previously indoctrinated crew members (Trusty Shellbacks) are organized into a "Court of Neptune" to indoctrinate the Slimy Pollywogs into "the mysteries of the Deep".[citation needed] Physical hardship, in keeping with the spirit of the initiation, are tolerated, and each Pollywog is expected to endure a standard initiation rite in order to become a Shellback.[citation needed] Depending on the Ocean or Fleet AOR, there can be variations in the rite. Some rites have discussed a role reversal as follows, but this is not always a normal feature, and may be dependent on whether a small number of Shellbacks exist to conduct the initiation.

The transition flows from established order to the controlled "chaos" of the Pollywog Revolt, the beginnings of re-order in the initiation rite as the fewer but experienced enlisted crew converts the Wogs through physical tests, then back to, and thereby affirming, the pre-established order of officers and enlisted.

The eve of the equatorial crossing is called Wog Day and, as with many other night-before rituals, is a mild type of reversal of the day to come. Wogs—all of the uninitiated—are allowed to capture and interrogate any shellbacks they can find (e.g., tying them up, cracking eggs or pouring aftershave lotion on their heads).[citation needed] The wogs are made very aware of the fact that it will be much harder on them if they do anything like this.

Neptune and his entourage during a Polish line-crossing ceremony (Chrzest równikowy)After crossing the line, Pollywogs receive subpoenas [4] to appear before King Neptune and his court (usually including his first assistant Davy Jones and her Highness Amphitrite and often various dignitaries, who are all represented by the highest ranking seamen), who officiate at the ceremony, which is often preceded by a beauty contest of men dressing up as women, each department of the ship being required to introduce one contestant in swimsuit drag. Afterwards, some wogs may be "interrogated" by King Neptune and his entourage, and the use of "truth serum" (hot sauce + after shave) and whole uncooked eggs put in the mouth. During the ceremony, the Pollywogs undergo a number of increasingly embarrassing ordeals (wearing clothing inside out and backwards; crawling on hands and knees on nonskid-coated decks; being swatted with short lengths of fire hose; being locked in stocks and pillories and pelted with mushy fruit; being locked in a water coffin of salt-water and bright green sea dye (fluorescent sodium salt); crawling through chutes or large tubs of rotting garbage; kissing the Royal Baby's belly coated with axle grease, hair chopping, etc.), largely for the entertainment of the Shellbacks.

Once the ceremony is complete, a Pollywog receives a certificate [5] declaring his new status. Another rare status is the Golden Shellback, a person who has crossed the Equator at the 180th meridian (International Date Line). The rarest Shellback status is that of the Emerald Shellback (USA), or Royal Diamond Shellback (Commonwealth), which is received after crossing the Equator at the Prime Meridian.[6] When a ship must cross the Equator reasonably close to one of these Meridians, the ship's captain will typically plot a course across the Golden X so that the ship's crew can be initiated as Golden or Emerald/Royal Diamond Shellbacks.[citation needed]

The University of Virginia's Semester at Sea Program holds a line-crossing ceremony twice a year for its students when their vessels cross the equator.

Criminal hazing: Raped by his fellow soldiers^

'Crazy Troop' NCOs court-martialed after initiation ritual in Iraq went too far, Army victims say

FORT HOOD, Texas — Minutes after returning to his room after a long day of training Iraqi soldiers, Spc. Jarett Wright heard the door open.

Three of his fellow soldiers entered and pushed him down on the bed. Wright struggled, but the other soldiers were too strong.

Two of them — both sergeants — held him down by the shoulders. Another grabbed his legs.

The soldiers ripped off Wright's belt and tore off his pants and underwear.

Taking turns, the sergeants grabbed Wright's genitals while the third soldier repeatedly shoved a finger into his anus.

The attack lasted about a minute. But Wright was not the first, nor the last, soldier in C Troop, 1st Squadron, 9th Cavalry Regiment, to endure this kind of assault. The unit calls itself "Crazy Troop."

Wright, who spoke to Army Times about what happened to him, said all the new guys in the troop experienced some sort of initiation. However, the initiations escalated with attacks on him and two other specialists, he said. The two other victims also described identical attacks in interviews with Army Times.

Army Times typically does not name victims of sexual assault, but Wright decided to speak publicly to try to prevent future attacks and insisted that he be named in the story.

"None of us wants this to happen to other people," Wright said. "If there's something good that can come out of this, [it] is prevention of that. I used to play football. I know what hazing is, I know what stupid stuff is. This is too far."

The cases against the soldiers in 1st Squadron stem from incidents that happened during a one-year deployment in Iraq from September 2010 to August 2011. After the attacks were reported, four soldiers were charged with crimes ranging from aggravated sexual contact to hazing, maltreatment and breaking and entering. Three of the soldiers — Sgt. Josue A. Nunez-Byers, Sgt. Brian S. Cornell and Sgt. Shane M. Newitt — have already been to court-martial. A fourth trial, for Spc. Benjamin Hill, is pending.

Defense attorneys for all four soldiers declined to speak with Army Times.

One of the specialists has been moved to a different barracks on post, but Wright still lives down the hall from Hill, who is not under any pretrial confinement, the soldiers said. Cornell is already out of jail and back in the unit, soldiers said.

The three victims plan to leave the Army within the next year.

The third soldier to be assaulted had seriously considered re-enlisting, he said.

"But once the trials started and we watched these guys walk, the level of stress was too much."

The first specialist to be assaulted and Wright, whose assault was the second to occur, both hope to someday return as commissioned officers.

"I was raped. I want to be discharged just to feel safe again," the first specialist said. "I need to be around people I trust. How can I feel safe with [a noncommissioned officer] when I was sexually assaulted by them?"

(In January of this year, the Justice Department changed the definition of rape to be "the penetration, no matter how slight, of the vagina or anus with any body part or object, or oral penetration by a sex organ of another person, without the consent of the victim.")

Wright said he needs some time away from the Army.

"I want to come back as an officer and hopefully make a difference," he said. "Justice wasn't done. I don't want them getting away with this."

Under newly created Army policy, the three soldiers could request to be reassigned, something they said they are considering.

Meanwhile, the 1st Cavalry Division, the soldiers' parent division, has launched a "thorough 15-6 investigation into these incidents, including actions taken or not taken by the chain of command," Fort Hood officials said. "Therefore, it would be inappropriate for us to answer [further] questions at this time."

But senior leaders at Fort Hood — where 1st Squadron is based — are taking reports and instances of hazing seriously, said Lt. Gen. Don Campbell, commanding general of Fort Hood and III Corps. Campbell ordered a post-wide stand-down in March, and hazing and the prevention of it was one of the topics he emphasized to his soldiers.

"It's a leadership issue," he told Army Times. "We can't look the other way. ... When hazing has been brought to the attention of any leader at III Corps, we have dealt with it in a very quick way."

The ongoing 15-6 investigation was requested by Col. Bill Benson, commander of the division's 4th Brigade Combat Team, and initiated by Col. Philip Battaglia, the division's rear detachment commander. The 4th BCT is the parent unit of 1st Squadron, 9th Cavalry Regiment. Battaglia has appointed an investigating officer from a different brigade, Fort Hood officials said.

Hazing an officer
Abuse at "Crazy Troop" was not limited to the three soldiers interviewed by Army Times.

Included in the investigation are snippets of video that show a junior officer from 1st Squadron being hazed by his fellow soldiers. Fort Hood officials aired portions of the video for an Army Times reporter.

In the video clips, the officer is duct-taped to a pole as several soldiers watch. He is shirtless, wearing only his Army Combat Uniform pants. Soldiers take turns pouring water on him, as well as packets of flavored drink mix. At the end of one segment of video, one of the soldiers grabs at the officer's pants near the groin, and the officer is seen pulling a handful of an unidentifiable substance from inside his pants. Wright and the other victims interviewed by Army Times said the officer in the video is a captain who was subjected to the same anal penetration that they were.

Fort Hood officials declined to identify the officer being hazed or the other soldiers in the video or comment on whether anyone was disciplined for the incident.

Citing the 15-6 requested by Benson, the Army also did not respond to questions about whether the chain of command within 1st Squadron was being investigated, whether the

142

command climate was being examined, or if any leadership within the unit might be disciplined in connection with the assaults on the junior soldiers.

They did note that the platoon, troop, squadron and brigade leadership have changed out since the incidents that were the subject of the courts-martial.

On March 22, Sergeant Major of the Army Raymond Chandler and the top enlisted leaders from the other services testified on Capitol Hill about hazing.

"Hazing has no place in our Army," Chandler said. "We will not tolerate hazing in any form, and we will hold those in violation of this policy accountable for their actions."

Since 2006, the Army has had 71 incidents or cases that meet the criteria for hazing, Chandler told the House Armed Services Committee's military personnel subcommittee. Those 71 cases involved 139 subjects and 123 victims, he said. Of the subjects, at least 65 received some sort of punishment, while 43 are still pending adjudication. No action was taken against the other 21 soldiers, he said.

"The challenge for us is that there is no punitive or statutory title for hazing," Chandler said.

Army Chief of Staff Gen. Ray Odierno discussed hazing in remarks to the House Army caucus last month. "In some cases, it is believed [the incidents] start out as something that is an initiation or fun, but they get too carried away. We are not going to tolerate hazing. "

Pain and humiliation
Soldiers from 1st Squadron, 9th Cavalry Regiment, deployed to Iraq in September 2010 and settled in at Contingency Operating Site Marez in Mosul.

Wright, who served in the Headquarters and Headquarters Troop, was moved to C Troop in March 2011. The two other specialists interviewed by Army Times also were transferred to C Troop during the deployment.

The soldiers said it was common for soldiers in the platoon to be subjected to the so-called credit card swipe, where soldiers would run their hands between a soldier's butt cheeks.

Another common occurrence took place when the soldiers would board a bus to get to their training site to work with their Iraqi counterparts. As a soldier boarded the bus, the soldiers already seated would jab their fingers up that soldier's butt as he walked by, they said.

According to the specialists, every junior soldier in the unit, at least E-4 and below, was subjected to some sort of harassment. However, the assaults continued to escalate, they said.

The first specialist to be sexually assaulted got to C Troop in March 2011. The soldier told Army Times he was in his containerized housing unit, sleeping, when Nunez-Byers, Cornell, Newitt and Hill burst into his room.

They ripped off his pants, began fondling and groping his genitals, and at least one of the attackers pushed his finger up the specialist's anus, he said.

"I was struggling, fighting the whole time, screaming for them to stop," he said. "It lasted maybe 40 seconds and they said 'Welcome to the platoon.'"

The specialist said he told his fellow soldiers what had happened, but that "this happened to everyone in the platoon. Everyone's scared."

In April 2011, Wright got back from a two-week leave. The specialist told Wright what happened and warned Wright that because he was new to the troop, he likely would be next.

For two weeks, Wright locked the door to his CHU and was constantly looking over his shoulder.

One evening, after a day of training, Wright went to use the restroom, then went back to his CHU but didn't lock his door. That's when the attackers pounced, Wright said.

The attack lasted about a minute, Wright said, but it was the most humiliating, degrading, traumatic and life-altering event of his life.

The third soldier was attacked in late April. He, too, had been home on leave, and was attacked three days after he returned to COS Marez.

All of the soldiers said they wanted to move past the attacks.

"I was the new guy, I wanted to put it behind me," Wright said. "But when you had time to process it, that's when everything started coming out."

On May 5, 2011, Wright turned 22. He was given a birthday spanking, which when described, it seems more like a whipping — 22 lashes, plus one extra for good measure, from a fellow soldier's belt. It left his buttocks raw and swollen.

"I couldn't lie down or sit for three days," he said.

In July, the birthday of the first specialist who was sexually assaulted rolled around, and he and Wright went into hiding, fearing that he would face the same whipping Wright received.

That was the final straw for the young soldiers. The specialist went to a sergeant he was comfortable confiding in. The assaults were reported immediately, Wright said.

"It was called Crazy Troop, and they lived up to this," the specialist said.

The punishment
The courts-martial for three of the four soldiers charged in the assaults are complete.

Nunez-Byers received the harshest sentence — two years in jail, a dishonorable discharge, and he must register as a sex offender. He was convicted by a panel of officers of aggravated sexual contact and hazing, among other charges.

Cornell, in a military-judge-only trial, pleaded guilty to hazing, assault and maltreatment. He received 20 days of confinement and a reduction in rank to E-3. He was not, however, discharged from the Army.

Newitt was acquitted by a panel of officers. Charges against him included hazing and maltreatment.

Hill will be the last soldier to be tried. As of April 19, a trial date had not been set for Hill.

He is charged with three counts of aggravated sexual contact, three counts of conspiracy to commit maltreatment of subordinates, three counts of violating a lawful general regulation, and three counts of housebreaking.

All three victims said they believe the suspects are getting off easy and that the Army isn't doing all it can to protect or help the victims.

Campbell said he couldn't discuss specific cases, but his message is "very loud and clear."

"We're going to hold you accountable if it's substantiated that you're hazing soldiers," he said.

He also wants soldiers to know they have a duty to report suspected hazing.

"Soldiers should speak up," he said. "And leaders set the tone so soldiers are comfortable coming to you.

"I don't want you to be afraid of making on-the-spot corrections, but then ask yourself if it's really necessary to make a soldier do pushups and flutter kicks to make an on-the-spot correction," he said. "If it doesn't feel right, if it doesn't look right, it's not right."

^ Tan, Michelle. *Criminal Hazing: Raped by his fellow soliders*: Army Times. 25 April 2012.

The Continuum of Hazing

Hazing activities vary in severity and exist along a continuum. At one end are initiation and group-building activities that do not constitute hazing. At the other end are severe forms of hazing that can result in severe psychological trauma, permanent injury, or death. In between there are a range of activities that might be considered low to moderate-level hazing.
Below are a few important concepts related to the continuum of hazing:

The Reasonable Person Standard:

Where a given activity falls on the continuum is not simply a function of what the act looks like to an observer. That's because hazing impacts people differently. An action that one reasonable person might experience as mildly humiliating might be experienced by another reasonable person as severely humiliating. In other words, when hazing occurs there are objective and subjective realities, both of which matter when assessing the severity of that action.

The Vulnerability Standard:

Certain individuals are more vulnerable to given acts of hazing, perhaps because of past experiences. For example, one fraternity required new members to perform an "elephant walk" in which new members were stripped down to jock straps, blind-folded, and forced to parade around the house in a straight line while holding each other's hands between their legs. Objectively, a reasonable person might describe this as a very humiliating act. But for one new member, the act evoked memories of being sexually abused as a child. For this vulnerable individual, the act was also emotionally re-traumatizing.

The Grey Zone:

Some people find it difficult to determine when a given activity crosses over into hazing. If you are unsure whether an activity constitutes hazing, start by asking yourself a few questions:

1. Would you hesitate to describe this activity to your parents or the police?

2. If a videotape of the activity was shown on the news, would you be concerned that the group would get in trouble?

3. Would the current members refuse to engage in the same activity?

4. If you answer affirmatively to any of these questions, there is a good chance that the activity is a form of hazing.

HAZING IN PROFESSIONALSPORTS[22]

In pro sports, hazing is out of the shadows . . . and on the wane

The Cowboys and Jaguars are leading what appears to be a move among NFL teams to curb the often embarrassing, sometimes injurious initiation rituals. The trend has caught on in baseball and NBA too.

The lockout might not be the only thing that ended in the NFL. Hazing seems to be on the endangered list too.

The Dallas Cowboys and Jacksonville Jaguars recently curbed the decades-old practice of veterans' roughing up rookies, setting an apparent trend of limiting the embarrassing incidents involving first-year players.

There's a long tradition of rookies being tied to goal posts, singing off-key songs in front of teammates and donning silly costumes at training camp.

But is hazing now considered hazardous?

"There's not going to be anything demeaning in any way that a rookie has to do," Cowboys Coach Jason Garrett told reporters. "We don't believe in that."

Garrett was an assistant coach last season when Cowboys receiver Dez Bryant made national headlines by refusing to carry the equipment of veteran receiver Roy Williams.

In an era when rapid player turnover is common, rookies are increasingly put in position to contribute right away in the NFL.

In Jacksonville, where rookie quarterback Blaine Gabbert is the face of the future, hazing is being swept out the back door.

"The whole thing really had gotten carried away in recent years," Jaguars Coach Jack Del Rio told reporters.

There will still be an annual rookie "talent show" in Jacksonville, and players have to carry teammates' equipment, but no eyebrows will be shaved and no awful haircuts will be given.

In fact, there might not be a worse haircut than the Friar Tuck offshoot Denver quarterback Tim Tebow received as a rookie last year.

"Hazing definitely has a negative impact on people and their self-esteem," said Bob Corb, director of the sport psychology program at UCLA. "It makes it hard to feel inspired. It could affect your trust. Coaches are figuring out that how a player feels about himself, his teammates and his coaches will affect his performance. It's like 'Why are we going through this?' It's hard to see what's redeeming about hazing people."

The recent history of hazing runs from innocuous to injurious, and includes the NBA and Major League Baseball.

Clippers forward Blake Griffin was forced to wear a pink Dora the Explorer backpack to ferry teammates' sweat bands and socks. He laughed it off. Then he became the NBA's rookie of the year.

Minnesota Timberwolves forward Kevin Love said he had to sing "Happy Birthday" to teammates if the date fell on a home game during his rookie season.

Cincinnati Reds outfielder Chris Heisey found a schoolgirl outfit hanging in his locker late last season. It was picked out by veterans on the team for the rookie to wear on a trip.

Initiation incidents went a step further when New Orleans Saints rookies Cam Cleeland and Jeff Danish were injured after being gang-rushed by teammates at training camp in 1998.

Cleeland sustained an eye injury after being clubbed by a bag of coins, and Danish was hospitalized after being shoved through a window. Danish won an undisclosed sum after suing the Saints, an assistant coach and a half-dozen players for more than $650,000 in damages.

. . .

22 Bresnahan, Mike. *"Sports hazing: A ritual whose time has passed"*. Los Angeles Time. 22 August 2011.

Football is the king of hazing, given its ultra-physical nature and the simple fact there are sometimes a dozen rookies on a team.

There is anecdotal evidence that pro baseball has more hazing than the NBA, but it appears to be shrinking in the former, with schoolgirl costumes slightly more an exception than a rule.

"It's changed," Baltimore Orioles Manager Buck Showalter told the Associated Press. "In fact, I'm kind of glad it changed. I've never been a big fan of the whole thing."

Said former Florida Marlins infielder Wes Helms: "It definitely has calmed down over the years. Rookies are a little different nowadays. When I came up, you didn't say a word until you had two or three years in the big leagues. Now guys come up and it's like they're already comfortable."

Corb, the clinical sport psychologist, said he understood the need for rookies to prove themselves in games to earn greater respect. They should also stay after practice to work on technique and put in extra hours away from the field to learn the playbook.

Corb was even fine with a type of class system based on seniority, such as better locker position, but said the premise of hazing should be left behind.

"I'm not so sure the people who do it even enjoy it," Corb said. "I've never met Derek Jeter or Tom Brady, but they seem like good guys. I can't imagine they would enjoy conducting this rite of passage."

CASE HISTORY 1

Even Wayne Gretzky was hazed in junior hockey. Brian Gualazzi, one of the Great One's former teammates with the Sault St. Marie Greyhounds, recounted for the Edmonton Sun last year an initiation in which the veterans took the rookies' clothes rookies and stuck the new players in a car:

"So there were seven guys sitting in the car naked, including Wayne. We had it all set up with the police so, all of a sudden the paddy wagon pulls up and somebody knocks on the window (of the car). The police arrested them with indecent exposure."

Gualazzi said that while being hauled away, Gretzky uncharacteristically tried to appeal to the police based on his star status.

"He said, 'Do you know who I am? I'm Wayne Gretzky.' And the policeman said, 'I don't care who you are. Get in.' "

The team veterans later showed up at the police station and let the rookies in on the orchestrated prank.

"Those initiation stories are always intersting because most of them you can't tell," Gualazzi said.

CASE HISTORY 2

From the small towns of rural Canada to a college campus in Ohio to the mountains of West Virginia where the Boston Bruins assigned their prospects, Ryan Johnston has the distinction of having played hockey at every level of the game, from pee-wee to professional. He was hazed at every stop.

The University of Vermont team whose season was cancelled for hazing activities was stocked with players from prep school and Canadian youth hockey programs.

He does not find this to be coincidence.

"I've played a lot of different sports," Johnston said, "and there's more hazing in hockey than in any other sport. I don't know if it's because the sport is more blue-collar, or because a lot of guys are straight off the farm or whatever. But it's just one of those sports."

Hazing Ryan Johnston is no easy feat: He's 6-foot-5 and 230 pounds. He was enough of man-mountain even at age 15 to punch and kick his way out of an effort by the older players at Blenheim, a junior hockey club in Canada, to give him a rookie mohawk. Other times he raised no objection, such as when he skated onto the ice before a game and a half-empty arena wearing nothing but a jock strap.

His experiences are far from uncommon. The cancellation of the University of Vermont hockey season in January put a national magnifying glass on the team's initiation rituals and brought embarrassment to the school itself. But current and former players at all levels told ESPN.com that the type and severity of the activities that the Vermont upperclassmen asked the freshmen to engage in are nothing new to hockey.

If anything, hazing is more pronounced at the youth levels, Johnston and others said. Among the reasons:

The top youth hockey players often move away from home before they graduate high school, whether to junior hockey programs in Canada or prep schools in the U.S. Away from their traditional support systems, they are vulnerable to the wishes of team veterans, who typically orchestrate hazing rituals.

Hockey players in those situations spend an inordinate amount of time with their new teammates, on the ice, in social settings and on buses traveling to games. Simply dressing and undressing in the locker room takes more time in hockey than in other sports that require players to wear less gear.

A lack of responsible supervision on the junior hockey level, where the teams often are owned by local businessmen and the players lionized in the small towns they represent.

Elements from all of the above came together in 1994, when 13 members of the Tilbury Hawks, a junior C team in the Ontario Hockey Association, were charged with 135 criminal violations, including multiple counts of sexual assault and sexual exploitation. They were cited for their involvement in an initiation party that included group masturbation, the shaving of pubic hair, and forced drinking.

The Tilbury players were told to do pushups and positioned on the floor so that their genitals would dip into cups of beer; whoever did the fewest pushups had to drink both beers. In another contest, the team captain placed marshmallows into the rectum of two rookies, with the last one able to push it back out being forced to eat both. Players also were blindfolded and told to lie face-up on the floor with their tongues out, as another person sat on their faces.

All of these alleged acts happened at the home of Dennis Lebert, one of the team's owners and a respected ear doctor in Chatham. In the end, team trainer Paul Everaert, 46, and team captain Ed Fiala, 25, pleaded guilty to committing indecent sexual acts. Their punishment: a total of $6,000 in fines.

156

"The (hazing) you see in hockey is highly sexual," said Laura Robinson, author of Crossing the Line, a groundbreaking 1998 book on violence and sexual assault in Canada's national sport.

Robinson, noting that many young players are new to sexual experiences, argues that some of the initiation acts serve as a hidden way for players to explore homosexual urges. "I think the boys are curious about bodies, but because of their homophobia they had to turn it into something else" -- sexual forms of hazing, she said.

"I've seen kids quit because they were so scared of that happening," said one college hockey player in North Dakota who spoke to ESPN.com on the condition he not be identified. While playing junior hockey in Montana, British Columbia and Saskatchewan, he said he saw rookies stuffed naked into the bathroom at the back of team buses, and games of tug of war in which skate laces were tied around rookies' penises. He said he also players who had strings tied around their penises, which were then connected to a hanging bucket that other players threw pucks into.

"They think it's good for team-building, but there are other ways to do that," he said.

Ken Dryden, the Hall of Fame goaltender and current president of the Toronto Maple Leafs, said the only hazing he endured during his playing years was getting his head shaved at Cornell University, in 1966. But he knows that hazing can turn abusive in hockey, even when rookies seem to have given their consent.

"The question is how it's felt, not how it's delivered," Dryden said. "You guys (who haze) may do it with a smile on your face and a laugh in your heart, but do not assume that the other guy is feeling the same way."

Maturity can help negotiate those scenarios. By the time Johnston turned professional in 1996, with the Huntington Blizzard, an affiliate of the Bruins in the East Coast Hockey League, the only hazing that remained was being required to buy dinner for the veterans, he said. Even at Ohio University, he considered the hazing activities to be acceptable, mostly consisting of one big night of drinking.

For Johnston, now an executive with a technology finance company, the worst of it was left in youth hockey.

"Hazing is like fighting -- part of the game," he said. "Part of the game that people who haven't played it just wouldn't understand."

CASE HISTORY 3
Carolina Panthers – 2004

However twisted the practice of "innocent" hazing might seem, it certainly does speak about the rookies' character. Especially if they can't deal with the simple fun stuff that let's them know they're part of a club. The Carolina Panthers have a pretty standard tradition of making rookies carry vet's pads and sing songs on demand.

On the last day of camp, the rookies are "asked" to step out in front of the entire club and sing, dance, and generally just act like a jackass at the veteran's request. Then it's done. Well, linebacker Sean Tufts didn't think he had any more in him when this final test came around. In a hilariously not-tough demonstration, rather than face the music and swallow his pride with his fellow rookies, Tufts went...another route.

He hauled ass into the woods to hide. Which worked. For about 20 minutes. Football players may not be splitting atoms, but they're not likely to forget about a rookie that runs and hides from his fate. Predictably, Tufts made it back to the locker room later to change. And his team was waiting for him.

To ensure that he wouldn't run again, players taped him to a chair outdoors, drenched him with ice water and Gatorade, then left him outside to think about what he had done. Eventually, two fans came by to set the not-so-tough linebacker free. It doesn't sound like Tuft's dignity made it through the ordeal.

CASE HISTORY 4
San Diego Chargers – 2009

Another well-known staple of the NFL initiation process is the purchase of dinners for other players. San Diego takes this practice a step further by "strongly suggesting" that the teams 1st round draft pick takes the entire team out to dinner. This pic shows what damage can be done by 50 or 60 NFL players who are probably eating out of spite.

As the above article states, Larry English could've had it a lot worse. Shawn Merriman's bill for his rookie season was $32,000 bucks, which probably works out to about $500 per player. I'm still willing to bet their kicker just had a salad and an Evian.

However, there have been protests of this tradition. Everyone's favorite benchmark for disappointment, Ryan Leaf, wasn't a big fan of this obligation, so he decided not to spring for dinner. The players decided that he was going to pay one way or another, so they lifted his credit card and dropped $3,000 on dinner. Ryan got off light for that dinner, but as we all know, karma caught up with him and did more damage than any group of linemen ever could.

Rookies dressed as smurfs. Comical entertainment or hazing?

WORK PLACE HAZING

Workplace hazing incidents may lead to serious injuries at work, divide the workplace and prevent employees from getting their jobs done. Often workplace hazing incidents go unnoticed or ignored as harmless fun. Some employers assume that hazing is just a bonding experience. However, making that mistake may jeopardize the future of your small business. Incidents of hazing include employees engaging in reckless horseplay, social pressure to participate in unsafe acts, bullying, harassment and violence.

Employers looking to develop effective hazing policies must train their staff to recognize and confront hazing in the workplace. Team building exercises allow staff to work together to solve problems, increase communication and foster group reliance. It's your responsibility as the business owner to ensure all employees have access to a safe, respectful and harassment free place to work. Consider the following preventive hazing methods in the workplace:

1. Create a workplace hazing policy to ensure management and staff recognize incidents of what workplace hazing.

2. Reinforce your policy about hazing in the workplace with materials to show unsafe behaviors.

3. Build trust and help employees form bonds with team building exercises.
Develop and design workplace hazing policies
 Protect your small business by making it clear that hazing and harassment are unacceptable. Learn best practices and implement strategies that managers and employees can adopt.

Try: Consult workplace-bullying consultants Work Doctor for assistance with creating and following a hazing policy related to bullying. Use the workplace bullying audio conference from Business & Legal Reports to aid managers and human resources when respond to bullying and hazing reports.

Clearly communicate your workplace hazing policy

Keep staff focused on the consequences of hazing in the workplace. List unacceptable behaviors and post them for employees to increase awareness. Also use posters, materials and targeted training videos to show the danger in hazing incidents.

Try: Order and post posters against hazing in the workplace. Provider SafteyPoster.com offers several horseplay posters. Educate employees on workplace safety with the training video from InteractiveSafety.com. Teach staff the consequences of hazing with a course from The Human Equation. Handle workplace hazing to teach team building skills Small businesses often discover hazing in the workplace when employees are unable to communicate with each other. Team building exercises teach employees how to trust each other and forms group bonds without the danger and fear found in workplace hazing.

Try: Leadership Innovations offers materials to develop a supportive workplace. Customized team building exercises from the Boston University Sargent Center for Outdoor Education are offered onsite, through mobile GPS or in your office. •Protect your small business budget by disseminating hazing in the workplace information before it gets out of hand. Employees can file workers compensation claims for injuries caused by hazing.

•If you find hazing in the workplace you must act swiftly to address it.

CASE HISTORY 1
Blythe, CA

Ex-Guard Describes Hazing at Prison

In a lawsuit, he says he was punished for reporting incidents at Blythe. A lawyer for the state calls the man a willing participant.

Behind the walls of Ironwood State Prison in Blythe, correctional officers regularly hazed their colleagues and harshly punished those who dared report the roughhousing, a former Ironwood correctional sergeant testified Tuesday in Riverside County Superior Court.

Curtis Landa -- who is suing the California Department of Corrections and Rehabilitation, alleging that officials retaliated against him for reporting one of the hazing incidents -- gave jurors a rare glimpse into prison life at Ironwood when he took the witness stand Tuesday.

Both Landa and an attorney for the corrections department acknowledged that the incidents were common.

They ranged from the nonviolent, such as officers' covering telephone receivers with mayonnaise, to fights in which a group of officers restrained a colleague with tape as they punched and kicked him.

But attorney Patti Ranger, who represented the state prison agency, portrayed Landa as a "a willing and active participant" in the back-and-forth "horseplay" among officers.

She described Landa as "buddies" with the men he later accused of attacking him, adding that he chose to engage in "this fooling around at work" and was seen by colleagues laughing off the incidents.

"We submit to you that there was no retaliation," Ranger told the jury.

Landa said he was often afraid of what his fellow employees might do to him and quickly learned that reporting the hazing could derail an officer's career and jeopardize his safety.

Landa detailed a 1996 incident in which he hid in a closet to escape officers who came after him for hiding a colleague's pink furry dice.

The guards sprayed pepper spray and slid burning toilet paper under the door -- forcing Landa to put on a gas mask and goggles for protection, he testified.

But he never considered reporting it, he said.

"It was widely known you did not tell on the staff," Landa testified. "If you had a problem with a person, you dealt with that person."

Landa says his troubles began when he did report a similar hazing incident in 2000.

He was stabbed in his driveway a month and a half later by unknown assailants.

He says prison agency officials forced him to leave Blythe for a desk job in Sacramento where he says he was mistreated by his new colleagues because they labeled him a snitch.

Ranger said Landa had no reason to complain about his transfer to what she described as a highly coveted background investigations job and said Landa had requested the transfer for his safety.

. . .

Reston, Maeve. *"Ex Guard describes prison hazing"*. Los Angeles Times. 27 September 2006.

CASE HISTORY 2
American Company in Afghanistan

Some private security guards hired to protect the U.S. Embassy in Afghanistan say their contractor has allowed widespread mistreatment, sexual activity and intimidation within their ranks, according to the watchdog group Project On Government Oversight (POGO).

A spokeswoman for watchdog group POGO said hazing at a camp for security guards went "well beyond partying."

The group sent a letter to Secretary of State Hillary Clinton on Tuesday, and briefed reporters on its findings, which it said are based on e-mails and interviews with more than a dozen guards who have worked at the U.S. compound in Kabul.

The company -- ArmorGroup, North America -- has a security contract with the State Department to provide services through July 2010, and has been cited several times for shortcomings in the security required by the contract.

A U.S. Senate panel two months ago was critical of the State Department for not closely supervising ArmorGroup, after a series of warning letters from the State Department in the year leading up to the panel's inquiry.

When contacted Wackenhut, the corporate parent of ArmorGroup, a spokesperson there said the company would have a response Wednesday.

The U.S. Embassy said Wednesday it was taking the allegations very seriously.

"Nothing is more important to us than the safety and security of all Embassy personnel -- Americans and Afghan -- and respect for the cultural and religious values of all Afghans," it said in a statement.

"We have taken immediate steps to review all local guard force policies and procedures and have taken all possible measures to ensure our security is sound." Should initiation rituals such as hazing be allowed? Sound off below

POGO says two weeks ago it began receiving whistleblower-style e-mails, some with graphic images and videos, that are said to document problems taking place at a non-military camp for the guards near the U.S. diplomatic compound in Kabul.

"This is well beyond partying," said Danielle Brian, POGO's executive director, after showing a video of a man with a bare backside, and another man apparently drinking a liquid that had been poured down the man's lower back.

She told CNN that ranking supervisors were "facilitating this kind of deviant hazing and humiliation, and requiring people to do things that made them feel really disgusted." Watch claims that alleged hazing at the U.S. Embassy pose a threat to security »

"This is not Abu Ghraib," she said, referring to images and videos of abuse by U.S. military troops against prisoners held at a facility in Iraq. "We're not talking about torture," she continued, "we are talking about humiliation," by supervisors causing a breakdown of morale, and a "total breakdown in the chain-of-command."

In the letter POGO sent to Clinton, Brian wrote that the problems are "posing a significant threat to the security of the Embassy and its personnel."

Among the recommendations from the group: immediate military supervision of the private security guards, a review of whether the contract should be revoked, and consideration as to whether government forces should replace private security in a combat zone.

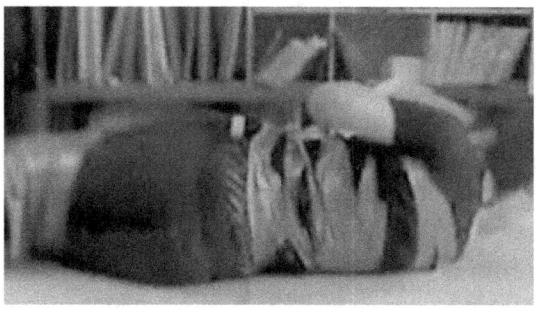

Five years after the abuse allegedly started, six months after the City of Mississauga began its own probe and two months after police were shown a damning video of mistreatment at work, Peel Region police are now investigating the allegations.

"We've started an investigation in light of the video, really," said Const. Wayne Patterson, spokesperson for Peel police. "That wasn't produced to us before. And, obviously, if you take the video alone and look at it, you would think that's more than inappropriate. The potential there is there's a criminal act going on."

But Alex Juani, who works in Mississauga's transportation and works department, said he showed officers the same video clip March 30. "It's the only video that I have and it's only one they have seen," he said, crediting the decision to investigate to the media uproar.

The tape shows two employees facing each other with their legs, hands and bodies taped up.

Though Juani claims the hazing had been going on for about five years, the city is sticking to its claim that it first learned about the allegations — that employees in the transportation and works department were tied up with duct tape, spanked until they were bruised and humiliated at the behest of one of their supervisors — only in November 2009.

City manager Janice Baker said the city's investigation concluded the "behaviour was in the nature of horseplay . . . locker room behaviour." Employees seen in the video were interviewed and did not file complaints, she said. "The discipline was not suspension or firing, it was extensive retraining around appropriate workplace behavior."

But Mayor Hazel McCallion said late Wednesday that firing the perpetrators hasn't been ruled out. She said she was referring the question of more stringent action to city council. Whether deemed simply "horseplay" or worse, such actions should not happen on city property and on taxpayers' money, she said.

In a news release Wednesday, Baker insisted the city had never been provided with a copy of the video and is "disgusted and appalled" by its contents. "We want to stress how seriously we took the allegations and that in no way do we condone this type of behavior."

Speaking to reporters before testifying at an inquiry on other matters Wednesday morning, McCallion said the city had called in an investigator immediately after the allegations were made. The March 9 report detailed several incidents:

• Two employees were bound face-to-face with duct tape on top of a large table in the sign workshop. Other employees then threw water balloons at them.

• An employee was bound with duct tape, put on the back of a truck and sent through a car wash.

169

• An employee, on his birthday, was told to lean over a table; other workers were instructed in turn to hit him, allegedly to "hit hard and to kick or punch in the face, ribs or groin area," the report said. If the blow didn't appear hard enough, they were told to hit harder.

The report said workers admitted that "practical jokes and hazing take place in the sign shop," but said it was all "appreciated, good-natured and voluntary."

One supervisor, Domenic Galamini, was disciplined. Galamini still works at the Mavis Rd. shop where more than 20 employees are based, installing and repairing street signs and painting traffic lines.

His wife, Viola, said Wednesday that Galamini was directing questions to the city manager. "He's not really speaking to anybody." The city is handling things because "it's already been dealt with," she said.

The Ministry of Labor got involved when an employee complained on April 16. It began investigating immediately and carried out an inspection April 19, ministry spokesperson Bruce Skeaff said.

"We were not called by the city of Mississauga," he said. "By the time we got there, the city had done their job and taken care of everything. They were in compliance and there were no orders issued."

Asked if the ministry couldn't take action for something as serious as hazing, even if it was no longer occurring, Skeaff said: "Basically we have to come in and find out for ourselves. The legislation isn't set up for us to act retroactively."

But Juani, 43, who has been on stress leave since October, dismissed the notion that the incidents were good-natured hazing, calling it "assault" and "harassment."

"I can assure you it's more than horseplay. It's oppression. We live under fear," he said, adding that he complained repeatedly to no avail. People were afraid of coming forward to report the abuse, he said, and fear compelled people to take part in hazing.

"It's so serious, we fear for more than just our jobs. (We) fear for our safety, safety of the people I love."

Adelino Botelho, who has worked at the plant 27 years, said he learned of the abuse months ago. "Everybody talked about it," he said. "My question is: Why didn't these (victims) fight back ... I guess they had no choice. They were overpowered."

. . .

McLean, Jesse, and David Rider. Police probe duct-tape hazing at Mississauga workplace. The Star. June 03, 2010

CASE HISTORY 4
NEW YORK, NEW YORK

James Jackson, a 26-year-old black employee of 180 Connect, was preparing for another day of installing cable, telephone and Internet service to residential customers of Cablevision in Nassau County, New York on December 7, 2007.

When he walked to the fenced-off area to pick up equipment for the day's jobs he looked up and was shocked to see a vicious, racist symbol in his workplace. A noose was hanging in the fenced-off equipment area, visible to the dozens of installers, the majority of whom are black, but accessible only to his boss and an equipment manager, both of whom are white.

Jackson, a former messenger who had worked at 180 Connect for a year and a half, immediately confronted the equipment manager, Dave Willie.

"I asked Dave," Jackson told CNN, " 'What is that hanging up there?' and he said, 'That is a noose' and I said, 'I know it's a noose, but why is it up there?' And he walked away."

Jackson and his co-workers say they were distraught.

"I just wanted to leave. I wanted to get out of there," 180 Connect employee Ralph Satterwhite stated. "I was disgusted."

The installers say they never complained to Human Resources. Instead, they consulted with a labor attorney, documented the incident, and decided to file a complaint with the Equal Employment Opportunity Commission.

Installer Shomari Houston, according to the complaint, says he asked his white boss, Gary Murdock, why a hangman's noose was in his workplace. He says the response was: To hang two black employees.

"He said, 'Yo, I like that, it's cool, I am gonna hang Russell up there. Think we can get James up there?' " Houston recalls Murdock saying. "I looked at him like, 'You serious.' "

Jackson says he continued to ask that the noose be taken down, and openly recorded the following conversation with Willie.

Jackson: "Who's that for, the rope?"

Willie: "For anybody who goes past that door that I don't want them in there."

Jackson: "Hang 'em?"

Willie: "Yeah."

Company says it has no tolerance for racism

After a week of complaints, the noose finally came down. The next day, December 14, the installers went public with their gripe, announcing their plans to file the EEOC discrimination claim.

180 Connect says it has zero tolerance for racism.

"It's inappropriate to put up any sign of violence in the workplace," said 180 Connect attorney Joel Cohen. "The company is aware that a noose could have racial connotations and could be a very negative symbol to African-American people.

"The company does not tolerate racism in the workplace and if anybody in the company engaged in wrongdoing, that will be dealt with and will be dealt with in a responsible way."

180 Connect has suspended Willie with pay, pending results of an investigation.

In a statement, Willie told CNN, "I am deeply saddened that a few of my co-workers have chosen to publicly air allegations of racism which they know to be false."

Willie's attorney, Richard Gertler, says his client's comment had no racial intent.

"He was saying it tongue in cheek. It's taken out of context," said Gertler.

Willie, Gertler stresses, is no racist. "My client's first marriage for 17 years was to an African-American woman. So I don't think he's racist."

Gary Murdock continues to oversee the warehouse at 180 Connect. Murdock did not return CNN's phone calls.

180 Connect has retained former National Labor Relations Law Judge Edwin Bennett to conduct an investigation. The installers, however, are refusing to appear before the judge without their attorney, which the company is not permitting, arguing it is not a legal proceeding.

Although the installers don't work directly for Cablevision, they also named the cable operator in their suit, saying company employees saw the noose and took no action.

Cablevision stated, "We are deeply troubled by the allegations about 180 Connect's workplace. We expect 180 Connect to conduct a thorough and credible investigation, to cooperate with any external investigation, and to take any appropriate actions."

180 Connect has more than 4,000 employees around the country. Among the cable television companies it provides installation services for is Time Warner Cable, a division of CNN's parent company, Time Warner. 180 Connect's operations are almost all in the United States, but the company has its corporate headquarters in Canada and trades on the Toronto stock exchange.

. . .

Allan Chernoff. *"Employees find noose hanging at work"*. CNN NEWS 5 January, 2007.

AN INDEPENDENT ANALYSYS

Hazing is a process, based on a tradition that is used by groups to discipline and to maintain a hierarchy (i.e., a pecking order). Regardless of consent, the rituals require individuals to engage in activities that are physically and psychologically stressful.

These activities can be humiliating, demeaning, intimidating, and exhausting, all of which results in physical and/or emotional discomfort. Hazing is about group dynamics and proving one's worthiness to become a member of the specific group.

WHAT IS HAZARDOUS HAZING?
Hazardous hazing occurs when the traditions or initiation rites skid out of control and cause significant and lasting physical and/or psychological damage. When hazardous hazing occurs everyone in the group, including the perpetrators, (those who planned and carried out the actions) bystanders (those who watched and did not actively participate) and victims, (those who were receiving the hazing) may be psychologically traumatized.

The families of those involved, coaches and other supervisors may also be traumatized; even if they were not present during the hazardous hazing.

Their trauma may be evident immediately, it may be delayed for months or years or even decades.

WHAT IS BULLYING?
Bullying is an intentional act of aggression that is meant to harm a victim either physically or psychologically. Bullies usually operate alone or in small groups and choose to victimize

individuals who they perceive as vulnerable. Victims attract bullies by their small stature, their younger age, or lower social status. Frequently there is only one specific victim who is often a scapegoat.

There are no traditions involved, nor are there authority figures or leaders.

The intent of the bully is to satisfy his own personal needs, such as obtaining money, lunch, homework or simply intimidating someone. Bullying has been observed in preschool children whereas hazing does not begin until middle or high school.

WHAT IS THE BLUEPRINT OF HAZING?
The blueprint of hazing states that the newcomer, or victim, is hazed. Once accepted by the group, the victim becomes a bystander, and watches as others get hazed. Eventually, the bystander achieves senior status and power, and becomes a perpetrator.

They do onto others what was done to them, and they feel as though they have the right and duty to pass on the tradition. High school students pack up this blueprint and stuff it into their backpack, in order to take their hazing experience with them to college, the military and the workplace. Each hazing brings with it the possibility of a new twist. Perpetrators want to leave their mark on the tradition, and therefore they may add or change the tradition, slightly.

When hazing situations go bad, those responsible are quick to say:

We never meant for it to end up like this...

We all had too much to drink and no one was thinking clearly...

The seniors initiated us when we were freshmen so we were just keeping the tradition going...

We were just trying to build a sense of team...

They could have stopped at any time, we weren't forcing them to do anything...

We would have never done it if we knew we could lose our season over this...

These are the typical things you hear from good, well-meaning teenagers and young adults after a seemingly benign freshmen initiation quickly and unwittingly mutates into a dangerous hazing ordeal that harms kids, threatens lives, destroys coaches' and administrators' careers, and tarnishes a team's and school's reputation.

Hazing is still a pervasive issue, especially in the athletic arena. It's often the result of newcomers desperately trying to fit in, veteran athletes who erroneously think they are promoting a sense of team, a lack of clear thinking because of alcohol, and the silence or absence of responsible leaders who know what is appropriate and safe.

As listed on the website stophazing.org, "a 1999 study by Alfred University and the NCAA found that approximately 80% of college athletes had been subjected to some form of hazing. Half were required to participate in drinking contests or alcohol related initiations while two thirds were subjected to humiliating hazing."

Further, as I travel around to various schools and get a chance to talk with student-athlete leaders, it alarms me that so many of them have a shockingly lax and innocent view toward initiation.

I hear things like: "It's harmless. It's great for team building. It's tradition. It was done to us."

Combine this permissive attitude toward hazing with the plethora of websites like Facebook and MySpace available for kids to post their party pictures on, and you've got the high likelihood of embarrassment if not disaster for your team/school.

In fact, the vigilante website Badjocks.com has made a name for itself by intentionally seeking out and posting any pictures related to athletes, partying, and hazing - raising awareness and accountability exponentially along with the stress levels of many coaches and athletic administrators.

The primary purposes of this article are to remind (and in some cases alert) you that hazing is still alive and well; that as a coach and administrator you must take this issue seriously, especially at the beginning of the school year when initiations are more likely to occur; and to offer some practical suggestions for proactively preventing hazing - or channeling it into more positive alternatives.

Reported Hazing Events *

*From Hank Nuwer, author of Recruiting in Sports, The Legend of Jesse Owens, High School Hazing, Broken Pledges, Wrongs of Passage, and The Hazing Reader

1923
Hobart College (New York)
Freshman Hazing

Two senior football players were expelled after freshman Lloyd Hyde was beaten and thrown into Seneca Lake. Three other senior athletes received lesser punishments.

1928
University of Texas (non-athletic hazing; included because death of athlete)
Delta Kappa Epsilon
Fraternity hazing (athlete involved)

Pledge Nolte McElroy, 19, a UT football player, died from electrical shock. Members asked him to crawl through mattresses charged with electrical current.

1975
University of Nevada, Reno
Sundowners (subrosa club heavy with athletes)
Drinking initiation death

Wolfpack football player John Davies died in an alcohol-related initiation. A grand jury blasted members but no one was charged with a crime.

1976
University of Texas
Texas Cowboys school-and-athletic spirit club

Members brained an initiate with wooden boards, and he was taken to an intensive care unit.

1978
Alfred University (New York)
Klan Alpine

Chuck Stenzel, a new pledge who hoped to join this fraternity which contained many lacrosse players, a major interest of his, died following a traditional Tapping Night for the chapter that included being locked in a trunk and given huge amounts of alcohol.

1979
Harvard University (Massachusetts)
Pi Eta

Paul Callahan, 22, a former Harvard basketball player, was paralyzed after a wrestling match which occurred following initiation ceremonies between new initiates and actives on a beer-coated linoleum floor.

1980
University of Michigan
Hockey
Alcohol-related hazing--severe

Michigan's athletic director castigated hazers ("Our practice is not to tolerate hazing in any form," said athletic director Don Canham) who shaved a player's pubic hair, stripped him, locked him in a trunk, drove around and then dumped him at a residence hall. He was drunk and covered with foodstuffs. Four others were initiated. It was cold, and an R.A. said the player had turned blue.

1980
University of South Carolina
Sigma Nu

Barry Ballou, who had been hazed in high school as a rookie football player, died following a drinking-related initiation run in part by an alumnus.

1981
Toms River, New Jersey
Soccer team tradition of initiating first-year players

Rookie soccer players said they were physically and vigorously pummeled during a long-tolerated school ritual known as "Freshman Kill Day."

1981
Wilmington High School (Massachusetts)
Football physical hazing at camp

Senior players allegedly urinated on younger players, a player told the Boston Globe. (Oct. 17, 1992)

1983
Nogales High School (Arizona)
athletic hazing court case

Seven junior varsity players from Nogales High School in Arizona said that they had been assaulted by older baseball players in the back of the team bus. Coaches were acquitted in 1984 court case but had to give up their positions.

1984
American International College (Massachusetts)
Local fraternity (heavily weighted with athletes)
Alcohol-related hazing death

Jay Lenaghan died in a 1984 marathon drinking hazing for his fraternity; many, like Jay, were athletes. Many were football players.

1985
Lowell High School (Massachusetts)
Physical hazing
Injury

After two hockey players suffered serious injuries, the school superintendent merely banned practices run by hockey team captains until the victim's parents protested, prompting five suspensions of veteran players.

1985-1986 season
Scotts Valley (CA)
Water Polo hazing

With the assistance of the Committee to Halt Useless College Killings, a Scotts Valley anti-hazing activist fought hazing after his son was subjected to physical and emotional hazing. He charged that water polo hazing could be tracked seven years. He said there were substantial gains, but he wanted hazing fully eliminated. (Files, CHUCK (Committeee to Halt Useless College Killings), Sept.
8, 1986)

1987
Evangel College (Massaxhusetts)
Minor hazing (with school sanctions)

Four football team starters were suspended for shaving the legs of a new player.

1988
Medford High School
Football camp hazing

Paul McGaffigan revealed on WBZ-TV that he'd been forced to run naked with a cracker between his buttocks as part of a traditional hazing game.

1988
Holmdel High School (New Jersey)
Improper Touching alleged
Football team

Football players were alleged to have been coerced into removing clothing and playing a game of Twister. The event was videotaped. The Bergen County Record on Nov. 12, 1989, said that "come coaches reportedly were disciplined." Players were taunted about incident by opponents.

1988- 89 season
Kent State University (Ohio)
Alcohol-related hazing
Close call

Tim Evans, a rookie hockey player, nearly died after veterans coerced him to chug liquor and beer through a funnel. Kent State President Michael Schwartz cancelled the school's hockey season. Five veterans were given suspended sentences and fines.

1988
Watertown High School (Massachusetts)
Football camp hazing

Numerous hazing incidents occurred at football camp. Three coaches and five players received suspensions. Some events involved humiliation and stripping and having a player sit in urine. (The News Tribune, October 7, 1988)

1989
Lyndhurst, New Jersey (high school)
Hazing
Football team

Leslie Weaver of the Bergen County Record reported that a high school sophomore football players was coerced into improper touching of another player while a large group (20-30) of players watched. The reporter wrote that the incident away from school took place at a Millersville, Pennsylvania football camp. The board of education responded by tightening academic requirements for players and banning secret societies.

1989
Pierce City High School (Missouri)
Football initiation

Source: students Eric Hartley and Maynard Moudy. On the first rainy day of practice, new players either wallow face-first in mud while grunting like pigs, or the juniors and seniors get to throw them in the slop. (Source: "Broken Pledges: The Deadly Rite of Hazing" by Hank Nuwer)

1989
Central Beurden High School (Kansas)
Wrestling initiation

Student Darrin Rierson said that the school wrestling team sometimes swirls the heads of rookies in a flushed toilet.

1989
Scottsville High School (Kentucky)
Baseball initiation

Student Danny Oliver said he played for his baseball team. The initiation he experienced was
getting held down while a player shaved leg hair. Several other clubs and band had no hazing—you
just joined and were in, said Oliver.

1990
University of Northern Colorado
Baseball team hazing
Serious injury

A slide into mud at the behest of some veteran teammates during an initiation left Kevin Wolitsky, 18, paralyzed. His neck was broken. News items at the time carried strong denials that hazing had occurred. UNC later disciplined the coach and players, according to the Denver Post. (See The Denver Post, March 15, 1998, etc.) The coach insisted the incident was "horseplay," not hazing. But a supporter of the Colorado hazing bill from UNC cited the case as hazing while lobbying for its passage.

1990
University of Texas
Texas Wranglers
Stealing as an initiation requirement

An initiate for this sports booster club was arrested for stealing a street sign he picked up while on a scavenger hunt.

1990
Western Illinois University
Lacrosse club drinking initiation
Death of rookie

Nicholas Haben died in a dormitory after being carried back to school following a drinking

initiation in a wooded area near campus. Twelve veteran participants were given community
service. The initiation had been going on for many years.

1990
Brockton High School (Massachusetts)
Track team

A rookie member claimed younger players had their underwear torn on bus and had traces of excrement rubbed on their faces and/or were made to eat pubic hair.

1990
Whitehall-Coplay High School (Pennsylvania)
Football

A rookie suffered a concussion after being beaten by twin lines of veterans.

1991
Jackson State (Mississippi)
Athletic hazing

Football coach W.C. Gordon took strong action by suspending four athletes and kicked two off the squad for allegedly hazing rookies.

1991
Delta State University (Mississippi)
Fraternity hazing by football players who were major part of group Ordeal for hazing

Two members of the DSU football team charged that they had been beaten in an initiation by three starters.

1991
The Citadel (South Carolina)
Athletic hazing decision

Four athletes who quit school and gave "hazing" abuses as their reason for leaving were refused "special case" permission to try to make the teams at another NCAA school. They were told to sit out one year (two years if they wish to play for a Southern Conference) team. The decision was made by Walt Nadzak, athletic director of The Citadel. Two players who protested the decision and reported hazing were defensive lineman Karl Brozowski and soccer player Michael Lake. Both were freshman athletes on scholarship.

1991
Ontario High School (Oregon)
Baseball team male-on-male violence

Police ended a one-year investigation into the sodomizing of four rookie players. Police said six veterans sodomized the four.

1992
Wilmington High School (Massachusetts)
Football physical hazing at camp

Police and administrators came under fire when some references to more serious types of physical assault were deleted from a written investigation report. Victims in the case claimed they were subjected to improper touching and physical assault, reported The Boston Globe (Oct. 17, 1992)

1992
Lodi (New Jersey) High School
Physical hazing
Financial settlement

Anthony Erekat, a member of the football squad, had his hair hacked off and had players spread feces and peanut butter all over his body during the initiation. He won a settlement.

1992
Sunnyside High School (Washington)
Hazing on Wrestling Team (sodomy)
Conviction

A young man, 15, claimed that he had been penetrated with a mop handle during an attack by several wrestlers. He suffered internal injuries. After plea bargaining, Richard Melendrez, entered a guilty plea to second-degree reckless endangerment.

1992
Johnson Creek High School (Wisconsin)
Taping admitted

Some wrestlers at Johnson Creek High School in Wisconsin admitted taping a student but denied sodomizing him with a mop handle as the victim claimed; they were acquitted of serious assault charges.

1992
Clintondale (Michigan) High School
softball hazing

Two female players removed a freshman teammate's ponytail with a knife.

1992
Golf club (Indiana)
Caddie initiation

A Ball State U. student, Mark Patterson, disclosed his regret at unintentionally breaking the arm of a new caddie when Patterson and another veteran caddie put a broomstick between the legs of the rookie to give him a ride as a type of wedgie.

1992
University of Western Ontario
Hazing allegation
Varsity football team

The London Free Press six years after the fact (November 1, 1998) reported that a high school coached warned the UWO athletic department that hazing was occurring. The coach reported that one of his former high school athletes quit the UWO Mustang team. The athlete said the hazing included coercion to steal, nudity, being pelted with food.

1993
Sky View High School (Utah)
Hazing and intimidation
Football team

School Superintendent Larry Jensen cancelled the last game of the football season and eliminated a playoff berth after a player charged that he had been taped nude to a table, mocked, and then subjected to having his female date see him in this state. The case was still in the courts in 2000.

1993
Glenbard West High School (DuPage, Illinois)
Hazing policy following physical hazing
Sports cheering squad

Administrators wrote a strict anti-hazing policy. The policy followed the physical hazing of Topperettes who were covered with bleach and other objectionable substances, plus talked into simulating sex acts.

1993
Haddon Township H,S. (New Jersey)
Football Hazing Reforms

Faced with hazing rumors they could not pin down, Haddon authorities instituted a hazing policy.

1994
Paine College (Augusta, Georgia)
Omega Psi Phi
Boxer alleges injury in physical hazing

Former Southeastern Golden Gloves heavyweight boxer Ric Ross claimed he suffered a spinal injury following a beating by members in a historically African American national fraternity.

1994
Shawnee Mission East High School (Kansas)
Soccer player hurt in school freshman initiation custom

The Kansas City Star (September 3, 1994) reported that the arms of two boys (one a soccer player who missed some games) were broken in a physical hazing ("hill rolling) ritual. The principal made an announcement that the custom was forbidden after the injuries occurred.

1995
Texas Cowboys
Athletic booster (spirit club) group
Alcohol-related drowning death in initiation

The Texas Cowboys, a spirit group that boasts members such as former Dallas Coach Tom Landry, held an initiation for so-called "Newmen" which included large amounts of alcohol. Gabe Higgins drowned in the middle of the night in the Colorado River. The
Cowboys were known for shooting the cannon during football games and for forming a sort-of honor line through which football players passed before each game. The team was put on probation and returned in 2000.

190

1995
High School in Hasbrouck Heights, N.J.
No action taken in initiation

Two seniors on the football team were not charged by police or punished by the school after asking two younger players to take a lap around the playing field without pants. Family members asked the police and school to let the participants settle the problem themselves.

1995
Wisconsin Heights High School (Wisconsin)
Athletic hazing

Five students were suspended for hazing rookies, including the taping of a player to a goalpost.

1996
Duxbury High School (Massachusetts)
Baseball initiation

Players were caught shoplifting items froim a dtore while dressed in varsity and JV uniforms as part of a team tradition. The team forfeited 13 games as part of its punishment. (New York Times, May 5, 1996)

1996
Azle High School (Texas)
Hazing (including cheerleaders volleball team members)

Two students were suspended and others apologized after a traditional initiation got out of hand, but fell short of qualifying as criminal hazing. The school acted swiftly to take action. (Star-Telegram, Sept. 9. 1996)

1996
Midland Lee High School (Texas)
Cheerleader allegations

A young woman charged that she had clothing ruined with substances in an unauthorized initiation. (The Houston Chronicle, Oct. 26, 1996)

1996
Salt Fork Storm (Jamaica High School and Catlin High School)
Alleged physical hazing
Football team

Joshua Lock, 14, told the Chicago Tribune (August 30, 1996) that his lacerated spleen was the result of hazing by an older player (and part of a pattern of hazing by older players).

1996
Buffalo Grove High School (Illinois)
Physical hazing General (male/female) student body (includes football team members)

A physical hazing supposedly got out of hand when overzealous bystanders lost control, according to some 20 older students who hazed 17 first-year students by spraying them with urine, cat litter, and hair-remover. (See Chicago Sun-Times, October 10, 1996)

1996
University of Georgia
Fraternity hazing of football player
Conviction

Running back Rod Perrymond was hospitalized with severe bruising after being paddled 50-70 times. He left Georgia because of a lack of playing time and a feeling of discomfort walking about campus. Three Phil Beta Sigma fraternity males pleaded guilty and were sentenced to perform community service but had all jail time suspended, according to the Atlanta Constitution.

1996
West Warwick High School (Rhode Island)
Football Incident

Whatever happened during an incident involving West Warwick football players is unknown, because the school district refused to tell a reporter, but a hazing policy was written after it occurred. (See October 8, 1996, The Providence Bulletin; "Wrongs of Passage").

1996
Santa Fe High School (New Mexico)
Football coach blasts student body for hazing

Stunned by repeated physical hazings and even a life-threatening alcohol initiation, administrators and coaches have begun speaking out. Steve Baca, varsity football coach, called the hazers "knuckleheads" in an interview with the Santa Fe New Mexican (October 5, 1996).

1996
Walla Walla High School (Washington)
Football hazing

Eight players were suspended from the team after a hazing incident at a Boise training camp saw six first-year players humiliated with improper bodily contact and having parts of their bodies coated with toothpaste. (The [Bend, Oregon] Bulletin, September 1, 1996). Fourteen players were reprimanded for not speaking out about the hazing they saw. Parents of the hazed students praised the school for its handling of the incident.

1996
St. Edward Catholic School (Chicago, Illinois)
Hazing allegations
Football Team

Five seventh-grade football players said they were bruised following a paddling by eight eight-grade players. "Isn't no big deal," the father of one eight grader told Fox TV News in Chicago.

1996
Hillcrest High School (Utah)
Football hazing

Five upperclass members of the football team were kicked off the team and suspended from school for hazing.

1996
Hempfield Area School District (Pennsylvania)
Football hazing
Injury

Nine veteran players admitted involvement after a sophomore football rookie was injured during traditional hazing. The school passed a hazing policy.

1996
Midland High School (Houston, Texas)
Cheerleader initiation

MHS cheerleading newcomer had chocolate syrup poured all over her school clothes.

1996
Alexander High School (Ohio)
Athletic hazing
No contest, conviction

The Columbus Dispatch, February 15, 1997, reported that football team captain Travis A. Hawk, 18, of Athens, "pleaded no contest to a misdemeanor charge of hazing involving several freshman teammates in the locker room showers in late October." Hawk was given a suspended sentence and $50 fine, plus community service requirement.

1996
University of North Carolina
Alcohol-related soccer team binge drinking

A rookie passed out in the home of a soccer team co-captain.The team was threatened with a forfeiture of games, and the school said it took a hard line on such activities. The team did some alcohol awareness-connected exercises on programs as a community service.

1996
Thorndale High School (Washington)
Football hazing

A junior-high player was brutalized with a plastic bottle by older players. The group apologized to the victim in juvenile court. (The Houston Chronicle, Sept. 23, 1998)

1997
Lifeguard hazing (Town of Babylon, New York)

Newsday journalist Michael Dobie wrote a 1999 article on the lifeguard initiation of Trevor Howard, 22, held two years earlier. Howard drank 17 shots and was incoherent.

1997
Holmdel High School
Soccer hazing

More than 200 people attended a Board of Education meeting after hazing reports surfaced. Many were angry that someone had complained about hazing. "Soccer is not a sport of the timid," a mother told the board, according to the Asbury Press (Nov. 7, 1997).

1997
Harvard University (Massachusetts)
Athletic hazing
Admissions made to newspaper

In a comprehensive look at hazing on campus, the Harvard Crimson (October 3, 1997) detailed numerous hazing behaviors such as so-called "voluntary" and coerced drinking, chugging from kegs of beer, eating of chili sauce, drinking at different stations, jumping off a diving board. Both male and female players were involved. Teams included women's water polo, men's swimming, and unspecified sports. Football players had whipped cream licked off their bodies as part of a cheerleader initiation. "Hazing and alcohol abuse will not be tolerated at Harvard," said Dean of the College Harry R. Lewis.

1997
Old Lyme High School (Connecticut)
Soccer
Hazing

Two male soccer players were suspended from school after a player reported that his pants had been sprayed with a chemical substance and lit in a hazing practice known as "butt burning."

1997
South Windsor High School
Hockey
Hazing

The school looked into allegations that new players were coerced into jumping off a ten-foot wall as an initiation.

1997
University of Washington
Soccer team
Rookie hazing

The men's soccer team under Coach Dean Wurzberger was given probation for hazing three rookie players.

1997
West Virginia University
Hazing allegations
Swim and diving team

Some team members were suspended for two meets after reports of coerced rookie drinking in conjunction with calisthenics was reported. A newspaper article said that the swim coach supported hitting hazers with penalties.

1997
Westlake High School (California)
Wrestling team

Seven wrestlers were suspended for hazing.

1997
Rancho Bernardo High School (California, Poway School District) Physical hazing and sexual assault
Junior varsity baseball player

After a rookie baseball player was sodomized with an object in the locker room, he settled for $675,000 with the district, according to

the San Diego Union-Tribunel. Court records showed that the attack was part of a six-year pattern of
assault in several sports and was deeply entrenched in school athletics

1997
University of Oklahoma
Female Soccer Hazing
Lawsuit

Kathleeen Peay, a player, charged that her coach led an initiation in which Peay had to wear a diaper and simulate sexual acts. Peay sued. Her coach is no longer with Oklahoma. Source: ESPN

1997
University of Wisconsin-Stout
Baseball hazing
Suspension

Veteran baseball coach Terry Petrie was suspended for one year after veterans were accused of coercing rookies into eating goldfish on a team away trip.

1997
Highlands Park High School (Colorado)
Football team

Highlands suspended seven players after allegations surfaced that hazing occurred at a football camp.

1997
North Carolina Central University
Football player hazing

A hazing incident occurred outside a residence hall. Five football players participated.

1997
Joseph High School (Oregon)
Football players and male-on-male violence

The Vancouver Columbian (September 28, 1997) reported the suspension of two athletes following an attack at a football team picnic. About 12 players attacked a 10th grade player while riding in the back of a pickup driven by a coach. One player rubbed his exposed genitals against the boys skin, and another forced the boy to touch the older player's genitals.

1998
Culdesac H.S./Lapwai School District
Suit filed in an Idaho court in 2000

The Lapwai School District and eight employees have been sued following initiations which two victims and their parents described as "assaults" and mock "rapes."

1998
Potsdam State College (New York)
Female soccer team hazing
Alcohol-related

Eight veteran players found themselves in considerable trouble after coercing first-year players to drink at a team gathering.

1998
McMaster University (Canada)
Rugby and volleyball hazing
Forfeitures

Two varsity teams forfeited games following accusations of rookie hazing.

1998
St. Bonaventure University (New York)
Drinking incident
Women's rugby

The school cancelled the club's season following a drinking incident. The school said it was punishing the drinking and that hazing did not occur.

1998
Alfred University (New York)
Football hazing
Alcohol-related

Alfred University President Edward G. Coll cancelled one football game, expelled a veteran player, and suspended six others after an alcohol-related hazing on campus. The incident occurred 20 years after an Alfred University student died at Klan Alpine, a fraternity preferred by campus athletes.
In response to the athletic hazing, Alfred University conducted a survey ("Initiation Rites and Athletics: A National Survey of NCAA Sports Teams") that was published August 30, 1999.
The survey was funded by the Riedman Insurance Co. (Disclosure: I was a national advisor on this survey).

1998
Scituate High School (Massachusetts)
Football player suspended in unusual (likely wrong) interpretation of hazing

A football player who dropped a young man on his face, requiring stitches and dental care for the victim, was suspended from the football team even though the action was intended as a prank and was not connected to the team. (The Patriot Ledger, October 30, 1998)

1998
Mead High School (Spokane, Washington)
Female soccer players
Initiation

A local paper quoted a student who said soccer players were taped to trash cans.

1998
Leonia High School (New Jersey)
Football team "bullying"

When older football players ganged up on a younger player, school officials termed the episode "bullying," and definitely not hazing. However, in a positive step, Leonia officials drafted a strong anti-hazing policy that athletes sign.

1998-1999
University of Western Ontario
Hazing
Football team

Numerous reports of hazing on the football team were reported. Hazing included an objectionable scavenger hunt list, use of alcohol, sexually explicit reading matter, condoms. Coach Larry Haylor did not coach the final two games of the season. Members of the team apologized. What was interesting was how many high school football coaches reported that their former players had expressed strong reservations about initiations at UWO.

1998
Mesa Mountain View High School
Coaches suspended
Football "Punishments" Administered

Mesa school board suspended the new head football coach and two assistant coaches briefly for not abolishing the practice of players administering pink bellies that went back to the 1970s here, according to the Arizona Republic. The pink bellies were a punishment, not hazing per se.

1998
Palm Harbor University High School (Florida)
Baseball
Physical hazing

Five baseball players punched rookies on the team bus. One or more put a burning ointment onto one rookie's bare backside. Players received light punishment, 3-5 day suspensions. (St. Petersburg Times, March 11, 1998)

1998
Thorndale High School (Texas)
Football
Sexual assault

Four football players pleaded guilty to misdemeanor hazing after injuring a rookie's anus and delicate organs with a soda pop bottle.

1998
New Orleans Saints
Professional football hazing

After the New Orleans Saints conducted a 1998 hazing similar to a gang "jump-in," rookie Cam Cleeland was sidelined with an eye injury he sustained when bashed with a bag of coins and rookie Jeff Danish was sent through a window and hospitalized for stitches. In 1999 Jeff Danish's hazing suit (U.S. District Court in Wisconsin) against former New Orleans pro football player Andre Royal was dismissed. Reason: Danish's attorneys did not continue their suit.

1999
Great Neck South High School (New York)

A player was roughed up during a hazing, according to Newsday.

1999
Cato-Meridian High School (NY)
Hazing punished (football)

The football coach punished players for hazing infractions.

1999
University of Vermont
Hockey Hazing

The school ended the season prematurely for hazing.

1999
North Branch School District (Michigan)
Basketball hazing
Saginaw State camp

Two coaches were fired, a player was expelled, and six players were suspended after terroristic-type hazing practices occurred at an away camp.

1999
Middletown, N.J.
Football camp at Wagner College (Staten Island, N.J.)
Alleged head shaving and physical hazing

Prosecutors said they lacked evidence to support claims by a 13-year-old Middletown
boy who said he had been hazed at a non-mandatory football camp this summer.

1999
Kalaheo H.S. (Hawaii)
Female soccer team

Two coaches were suspended after girls were made to run around a field in underclothing.

1999
Prospect High School (Illinois)
Football team
Controversy
A freshman football player said he had endured hazing. Veterans called it horseplay.

1999
Chicago Bears (Illinois, professional)
Football hazing

After a coaching edict forbade hazing, players carried out an initiation anyway. No punishment followed.

1999
Stevenson H.S. (Illinois)
Football hazing

Officials suspended four players for so-called atomic situps that involve ridicule and humiliation. Sports Illustrated ran an article "In Praise" of such hazing and failed to print letters from parents whose children had been injured or tormented in hazing incidents.

1999
Raoul Wallenberg Traditional Alternative High School (California)
Baseball
Sexual assault investigation

The San Francisco Examiner reported that school officials and police authorities are investigating a possible "sexual assault by high school baseball players on younger Teammates while at a tournament." The coach was fired immediately.

1999
Aiee High School (Hawaii)
Soccer   (charges filed)

A player was assaulted by six teammates after refusing to let them haze him.

1999
McAlester High School (Oklahoma)
Football physical hazing
Injury

Matt Warnock suffered a head injury after he was jumped by teammates in a locker room hazing by teammates. It was the second hazing injury involving the football team in two years.
The incident angered the mother who demanded that the football team be shut down, just as fraternity chapters are closed when members are caught hazing.

1999
Hinsdale H.S (IL)
Baseball hazing

Three players faced battery charges after forcibly cutting a player's hair.

1999
North Thurston School District (Washington)
Study underway

A study on student behaviors resembling hazing and other related behaviors is being conducted at North Thurston School District in Washington. The school had a football team hazing incident.

1999
Georgia Southern University
Baseball Hazings alleged

Several players were suspended in the aftermath of a hazing investigation. Players complained the school made them scapegoats.

1999
Ellicott City High School (Maryland)
Hazing by senior players

Senior players kicked balls at the rumps of junior high school players in an annual tradition known as butts up.

2000
Marian College (Wisconsin)
Hockey hazing

Coach Paul Caufield resigned after a hazing on the team bus, according to the Minneapolis Star Tribune.

2000
Newtown High School (CT)
Wrestling Hazing

A practice called "swirlies" (dunking a rookie's head in a toilet and flushing it) led to the forfeiture of four matches by the wrestling team.

2000
Hofstra University
Crown and Lance (mainly football players in this fraternity)
Hazing investigation launched

New York Newsday reported March 9 that Hofstra University suspended Crown and Lance fraternity scheduled a Hofstra judiciary board hearing to look into possible hazing. Officials alleged that Crown and Lance, mainly made up of football players, may have been involved in some initiation ritual that involved five pledges and a sheep on a public beach. The police sent the group packing without charges and no alcohol was involved.

2000
Fort Madison High School (Iowa)
Minor infractions admitted (sodomy refuted)

The Des Moines Register reported that school officials said that an investigation found that a wrestler was taunted and taped by older players, refuting a claim by Fort Madison (Iowa) high school nurse who earlier alleged that a "rookie" wrestler was sodomized with a marker by teammates.

2000
Trumbull High School (CT)
Wrestling team

One new wrestler (a special education student) was injured, and several others allegedly were hazed, at Trumbull H.S. Six wrestlers face charges. Although police refused to identify charges publicly, a lawyer said the special ed student was forced to suffer indignities, including the insertion of a plastic knife into his rectum. Eight were suspended. Three veterans were arraigned in Bridgeport Superior Court on criminal-assault charges.

2000
Absegami (NJ) HS
Wrestling initiation

Labe Black, a wrestlerarrested for making a young wrestler chug alcohol as part of an initiation, was allowed by the school district to win a championship.

2000
Nazareth High School (Pennsylvania)
Athletic hazing (basketball)

Three coaches resigned and seven varsity players received one-week suspensions after a January initiation in which basketball veterans removed underwear of junior varsity players on a team bus. Coaches were present but failed to halt the hazing. Parents have come to the defense of the coaches.

2000
North Yarmouth Academy (Maine)
hockey hazing

Two players were disciplined by the headmaster after a hazing.

2000
Hilton Head High School (South Carolina)
Wrestling hazing

 Wrestling coach George Dixon resigned after a student said he had been sexually assaulted with a broomstick during an initiation rite.

2000
Einstein High School (Maryland)
Athletic hazing
Einstein High School suspended veteran wrestlers and forfeited one match after a rookie was hazed.

2000
Decatur High School (Texas)
Athletic hazing

The Fort Worth Star-Telegram reported an instance of athletic hazing in which two players were
severely bruised.

2000
Mansfield High School (Texas)
Athletic hazing

A football player beaten by veterans was treated for fluid in his lungs and quit school, according to the Fort Worth Star Telegram.

2000
Glendale School District (CA)
Athletic hazing

A coach resigned in the wake of athletic department allegations involving acts of sodomy with a small bat and broom handle.

St. Michael's College (Canada)
Football Hazing
Nudity, physical hazing

 Five players apologized after taping an unclothed player to a goalpost and smashing eggs into him.

University of Maryland
Athletic Hazing
Investigation concluded
2000

The University of Maryland investigated several hazing allegations and decided hazing had occurred.

University of Brunswick (Canada)
Rugby (close call--alcohol)
Hazing
2000

A 17-year-old rugby player survived with blood alcohol content FIVE times the legal intoxication level. He was hospitalized and is expected to live. The school has suspended the team while investigating the incident. No arrests have been made or announced.

2000
Yale University
Athletic hazing charges and denials

Allegations of hazing were levied against the heavyweight crew team, leading to a team suspension. The team was found innocent by the Athletic Department after two first--year members were taken to health services because of severe intoxication. There was confusion on campus as several other squads, including the men's swim team, had members declare that they participated in voluntary initiations. The Athletic Department has strict rules against hazing.

2000
Elkhart Memorial High School (Indiana)
Swim team lawsuit

Sam Lentine, a new member of the swim team, alleges that his head was shaved and cut by another athlete. When he went to the school's athletic authorities, alleges Lentine, he was told that the head shaving was part of team tradition.

2000
Winslow High School (Arizona)
Sexual hazing alleged (basketball/track)

Members of a girl's athletic squad charged that they saw evidence of male athletes being sodomized with fingers and objects. A parent of a young man accused of hazing says due process was not followed. Basketball coach Daniel Gonzalez was indicted on three felonycounts of child abuse.
.

Eastern Randolph H.S. (North Carolina)
Hazing injury: Football rookie

The school's football coach is paying for the medical costs of treating a freshmen player who has a bruised ear and a slight concussion following a traditional rookie pillow fight.

Moon Area High School (Pennsylvania)
Football hazing and coverup

After a football player suffered a concussion after being belted with an alarm clock in a hazing incident, team members tried to make up a story to cover up the incident, the school confirmed. "One [player] said the thing about going to camp [for an initiation] is to pull together as a team. This whole thing has splintered us, " Coach Mark Capuano told the Pittsbugh Post-Gazette.

New Richmond High School (Wisconsin)
1999-2000 hockey team
Season forfeited for hazing

The team forfeited four games after a player was taped by teammates.

Spartan Youth Football program (WI)
Hazing charged and denied
youth football
2000

A player had his arm broken. There is a dispute as to whether hazing or discipline was the cause.

Lansing High School (KS)
Soccer
hazing
2000

Varsity soccer players were arrested for alleged physical hazing.

Cibola High School (NM)
physical hazing
Athletic hazing allegations under investigation
2000

Five Cibola students have been suspended for hazing, said Cibola coach Ben Shultz, who declined to name the athletes and non-athletes.

North Hardin High School (Kentucky)
Cheerleader hazing (lawsuit)
2000

The Louisville Courier-Journal revealed hazing allegations by two girls alleging physical restraint, abusive behavior and verbal abuse. The two filed
a lawsuit in Hardin County District Court.

Yucca Valley High School (California)
Football hazing
Hazing and rape alleged
2000

At least two victims claim they were hazed and raped in a hazing initiation. Charges werebrought against numerous senior members of the football team, dividing this quiet community into camps of supporters of the victims and antagonists saying racism was a factor. Six were expelled.

El Dorado High School (CALIF)
Non-Criminal Athletic Hazing
Football team
Nov. 2000

School authorities suspended seven starters for a videotaped incident in which a student was shoved in a locker. The coach subsequently was let go by the principal.

Mohawk High School (Ohio)
Wrestling team
Hazing
2001

Six wrestlers served out suspensions for hazing.

El Dorado High School (California)
Coach fired, blames hazing
2001

Twelve-year veteran coach Rick Jones says he was fired after he reported a non-criminal hazing incident. The school says other factors were involved.

University of Minnesota, Duluth
Rugby death
Men's and women's rugby initiation
Ruled an accident
2001

Although Ken Christiansen had been drinking at an initiation party and veteran members scrawled pictures on their faces, he died of an accident when he fell dead drunk into a creek and died.

Grants High School. (New Mexico)
Athletic Hazing leads to expulsion
2001

The school suspended one student and kicked out another after alleged hazing occurred on the baseball squad. Two victims were hazed, and a 19 year-old pleaded guilty to indecent exposure.

Lookout Valley High School.(Tennessee)
Criminal Hazing Alleged.
Athletic Hazing allegations (Lookout Valley baseball team)
2001

Michael Shaun Long, 18, was charged with sexual battery assault, but the charge was reduced to indecent exposure. The charge is that he participated in a hazing for the baseball team in which a 16-year-old boywas forced to accept a player's genitals on his face. Long's attorney plans to argue his client released the victim, unaware the other person planned to expose himself. There also is conflicting testimony by witnesses as to whether or not the victim was actually touched by the supposed assailant.

Palm Harbor University High (Florida)
Principal Says Incident was Rough-housing, not hazing
Baseball Team Incident
2001

Alec Liem, Palm Harbor University High principal, says an incident in a FortLauderdale hotel where players jumped on another player is not a case of hazing, but rough-housing. The Pinellas County Sheriff'sOffice earlier had said it was investigating whether hazing had occurred.

Holden School (Louisiana)
Non-criminal Athletic Hazing
Basketball team
2001

The Holden School decided on education instead of punishment after sixth graders were given pink bellies by the veteran basketball players as a greeting. The coach was unaware of the ritual. No one was injured.

.Alexandria High School (Louisiana) Update on 2000 case
Athletic hazing with injuries
Civil lawsuit (June)
2001

The mother of new football player Trey Warner III is suing for $50,000, seeking damage for a broken nose and other head injuries. He was beaten in the locker room.

Update on earlier case (1999 incident)
Athens High School (Texas)
Civil Suit Alleges Hazing and Inaction by school district

Tommy and Susan Stutts of Athens and their son filed a suit that said the school and its officials improperly handled an incident in which he allegedly was jumped and hazed on a team bus.

Andrew High School (Iowa)
Athletic Hazing (basketball) alleged
2001

An alleged basketball hazing made victims uncomfortable at their old school. One player who transferred
to Bellevue Marquette was allowed to do so without any eligibility penalty as a result of his victimization.

Colgate University
Athletic Hazing
Past Incidents Revealed in Book

Former goalie Ken Baker claimed the team's rituals included beatings, shaving of pubic hair, and heavy drinking. The claims were made in his new book published by Tarcher.

Northern Highlands H.S. (N.J.)
Athletic hazing (female field hockey)
2001

14 players have lost team status after younger players said they'd been subjected to sexual simulation acts and demeaning activities. Lawyers for some of the parents said they will sue to get daughters back on team.

Eustis High School (Florida)
Junior HS Football Hazing
Under Investigation (Oct 2001)

A school principal was temporarily removed as investigation is under way.

Buffalo Grove High School (Illinois)
Chicago suburb
Hazing Suspensions (Nov 2001)

Thus far 12 upperclass students have been suspended in a hazing incident. Some under investigation are football players.

Sycamore High School (DeKalb, Ill)
Hazing allegations
Football team

Allegations of improper touching of athletes' bodies during a football hazing are being investigated by the school and police, according to the Daily Chronicle newspaper.

Pinkerton Academy (New Hampshire)
Internal investigation, hazing allegations (Dec. 2001)
Basketball team

Pinkerton coach Tony Carnovale says that a   "real minor situation" occurred while the team was at a
Comfort Inn in Hyannis, Mass.

Baldwin High School (NY, Nov-Dec 2001)
Hazing charges
Football team

Two seniors have been charged with first-degree sexual abuse and endangering the welfare of a child following the alleged hazing in a locker room before practice. The victim was 14. Other teammates have threatened the victim.

Averill Park High School (Sand Lake, NY , Dec 2001)
Hazing on Trial, allegations of tampering
Football

Five people (two teachers and three students) plead not guilty in hazing incident; (allegations were that a student dragged his genitals against a junior varsity player's face). Students charged with attack are William J. Schoonmaker, 17, George M. Krug, 17, and Vincent J.
Bowen, 17. The teachers charged with witness tampering are Thomas E. Katchadurian, 25, of East Greenbush and Amelia Costello, 55, of Brunswick. Trial starts in 2002 unless plea bargaining occurs.

Webster High School
Tulsa, Oklahoma
Sexual Hazing (Fall semester 2001)

   Tulsa Schools suspended fourteen students and cancelled the Webster ninth-grade football season after a 14-year-old student allegedly was held him down and raped with a broom handle. This was followed by whipping him with a weight belt. His genitals were beaten with traffic cones.

Pentucket High School (Mass.)
Sexual hazing acts alleged
Police investigation follows school "internal" handling of situation.

Football team

An alleged preseason hazing incident involving eight or more players at a football camp is now being looked into by police. AtCamp Marist in Center Ossipee, N.H., veteran players allegedly placed genitals in faces of players, according to an investigation by the Lawrence (Mass.) Eagle-Tribune reported. One coach expressed surprise, saying the matter had been handled internally.

Schools do not have police powers, author of hazing books Hank Nuwer stresses over and over. All "interna;" investigations where a serious crime may have been committed should be turned over to police who are trained to investigate such matters.

New London High School (Madison County, Ohio)
Sexual assault allegation
Wrestling team (2002)

A 14-year old player's statement that he was sodomized with fingers by teammates is under investigation.

Alamo Heights High School (Texas)
Cheerleader Hazing and Alcohol
Case Appears to Be Headed to Court (2002)

Officials dismissed 15 of 16 varsity cheerleaders for alleged hazing and underage drinking. Parents at first countered with a lawsuit,saying males present were punished less severely. The suit was eventually dropped.

Las Vegas (NM) City SchoolsRobertson High School
Baseball hazing (2002)

The City Schools board of education failed to renew the contract of Robertson High School
baseball coach Dale Turner. He said a hazing
injury forced his departure, but the school gave no public reason.

1. New London High School (Madison County, Ohio)
Sexual assault allegation
Wrestling team (2002)

A 14-year old player's statement that he was sodomized with fingers by teammates is under investigation.

2.
Carson High School (Nevada)
Hazing Reforms Introduced by School

Summary from "Principal says hazing tough to stop at Carson High"
Ray Hagar
RENO GAZETTE-JOURNAL
1/22/2002

Principal Glen Adair told school board members Tuesday night that Carson
High School is winning its 60-year war on hazing.

"When it was initially started, it was really innocent," Adair said. "Itonly involved a few people and was fairly discreet.

"Now, we have young men that are stripped naked, we have young men who areasked to run down a hill and are shot with BB guns, whipped with troutrods, beat with belt buckles and everybody has a high old time."

Adair said such incidents happened at Carson High at least five years ago,but there have been no incidents this year and only a minor hazing incidentlast year in which girls had shaving cream sprayed on their heads.

3. Alamo Heights High School (Texas)
Cheerleader Hazing and Alcohol
Case Appears to Be Headed to Court

Officials dismissed 15 of 16 varsity cheerleaders for alleged hazing and underage drinking. Parents have countered with a lawsuit,saying males present were punished less severely.

4. Greenville High School (Maine)
Hazing ended with policy (2002)

The school has ordered all hazing stopped. Previous hazing included making first-year students jump into an icy lake and race with Tabasco sauce in their mouths.

North Sanpete High School
Mount Pleasant, Utah
Shaving male cheerleader's pubic hair
January 22, 2003

Two wrestlers were suspended for 10 days by the principal after a male cheerleader alleged they had tried to haze him by shaving his pubic hair. One teen wrestler was given probation. An 18-year-old wrestler was fined $550 after entering a plea of guilty in Mt. Pleasant municipal court to a single Class C misdemeanor charge of assault, according to the Deseret News.

The school district was sued by the cheerleader's parents and settled for an undisclosed amount.

Attica High School
Attica, New York
Urine splashed on basketball players as initiation
February 2003

One player was charged for hurling basketballs at players, while an 18-year-old player was charged with four counts of battery by body waste, three counts of battery causing bodily injury, and three counts of battery. That player in turn criticized school officials, saying he himself had been subjected to beatings and being covered with urine as a first-year player. Three veterans were each given one-year probation sentences by a court.

Kirtland High School
Geauga County, Ohio
Summer camp counselor hazing alleged
2003 (investigation carried over into 2004)

A 17-year-old counselor was charged with hazing after exposing himself and requiring younger campers to perform situps that brought him into the vicinity of his bare buttocks. A prosecutor blasted Kirtland administrators for failure to cooperate with the investigation for more than eight months, according to the Cleveland Plain Dealer. The incident came to light when a mother visited the camp and saw the alleged hazing.

Glenbrook North High School
North Brook, Illinois
Powderpuff football game by females
May 2003

Older students pelted younger females with waste and other substances in a widely viewed hazing on CNN that was fueled by alcohol purchased by some parents of the hazers.

Brecksville-Broadview Heights High School
Broadview Heights, Ohio
Finger inserted during hazing (charges reduced)
May 28, 2003

As part of a hazing practice done to freshman and sophomores, two teens held down a 16-year-old while a third teen put one finger into the victim's anus. Patrick Pristas, 18, pleaded guilty to a reduced charge of assault and unlawful restraint and was put on probation.

North Carolina State University
Raleigh, North Carolina
sodomy
2003

After a lengthy investigation, two Avery County basketball players working at an NCSU basketball camp admitted sodomizing younger students in a dormitory, according to the Raleigh News & Observer. One was found guilty of ten counts of hazing and the other was guilty of multiple accounts of simple assault. One was expelled from Avery and both were kicked off the basketball team. The two were placed on probation and ordered to stay away from the victims. A father told the newspaper is son's rectum was severely injured. The families of the victims cooperated with the court to let the more culpable offender receive a misdemeanor charge instead of a felony charge that brought with it far tougher sentencing. Avery basketball coaches were supposed to be supervising the counselors.

Fulton School District
Fulton, New York
Alleged sexual hazing
2003

Four junior high football players were accused of terrorizing younger players by holding them down and sexually attacking them, according to the Syracuse Post-Standard.

W.C. Mepham High School
Bellmore, N.Y.
Football Camp
2003

Veteran football players penetrated three JV players with a broomstick, pine cones and golf balls during several attacks. Two coaches lost their job and were reassigned without teaching duties. Two players were sentenced to serve time in detention centers. Two others received probation.

Savannah-Country Day School
Savannah, GA
Cheerleading
Possible hazing incident (sexual)
August 4, 2004

Members of the Country Day school cheerleading squad were reportedly told to commit humiliating and sexual natured acts by other squad members. An investigation began following rumors of the incident. Five members were expelled from school.

Groton School
Groton, Massachusetts
Sexual hazing offenses
2004

Cannon "Zeke" Hawkins and other students came forward to report sexual hazing and exploitation of younger students by upperclassmen. He and others had their genitals groped. The Trustees of the Groton School pleaded guilty in 2005 to a failure to report the child abuse allegations as Massachusetts law required, according to the Lowell Sun.

Central Cabarrus High School
Charlotte, North Carolina
Indecent liberties during hazing
May 2004

Although a school spokeperson refused to divulge details of an alleged hazing attack, the school superintendent told the Winston-Salem Journal that three baseball players were suspended for taking "indecent liberties" during a hazing incident. No other details were available.

Lassiter High School
Marietta, Georgia
Hazing with sexual battery
March 2004

The Atlanta Journal-Constitution reported that three students had been charged with sexual battery offenses following two hazing incidents. The district cancelled the remainder of the season.

Leavitt Area High School
Turner, Maine
Senior paddling
March 2004

Administrators punished seniors for whacking incoming students with paddles. No one was charged. No injuries were reported.

225

Roselle Park Middle School.
Roselle Park, New Jersey
Basketball initiation with simulated homosexual sex acts
March 2004

The Star-Ledger of Newark reported that four players were inappropriately touched with body parts by two 15-year-old players. The matter was tuned over to juvenile authorities following complaints. The newspaper did not know the specific charges that were filed.

Glenbrook South High School
Glenview, Illinois
Paddling and alcohol use
April 2004

Authorities said 11 lacrosse members paddled 13 newcomers to the team.

Camp Lohikan (Pennsylvania)
West Morris Regional School District
New Jersey
Nude skits at football camp
2003-2004

Coaches were admonished after sophomores were asked to put on skits for the entertainment of older players. Skits included nudity and covering of a naked player with food substances. The news of the skits reached administrators months after the camp ended.

Hastings High School
Hastings, MN
Senior-freshman paddling
June 2004

Six seniors at the high school were charged with assault after beating incoming freshmen with hockey sticks. At least two enter guilty pleas to misdemeanor assault.

West De Pere High School
De Pere, WI
Sexual hazing by urination
September 2004

Younger students of the high school were hazed by older students during homecoming activities. The incident involved the students being taped to poles and sprayed with shaving cream. Others were urinated on, according to the Green Bay Post Gazette.

Buena High School
Sierra Vista, AZ
Volleyball player hazing (sexual)
May 6, 2004 (reported)

A 16-year-old volleyball player was assaulted by an older member of the team while on the bus drive home after a game. The 16-year-old was held down by other team members while the 17-year-old hit the younger member over the head with his penis. Four team members were arrested.

Webster County High School
Dixon, KY
Sexual natured hazing
May 5, 2004

Three 18-year-old students sexually hazed a 14-year-old student in a Webster County High School locker room. Two of the upperclassmen pinned the 14-year-old down and the third pulled down the boy's pants and touched his buttocks. All three students are faced with charges of sexual abuse.

North High School
Fargo, ND
May 2004

This incident occurred on the last day of school as upperclassmen paddled freshman students. Five students who committed the act were suspended from school. Alcohol was reportedly involved.

Roane County High School
Kingston, TN
August 2004

In this incident, freshmen students were reportedly beaten by upperclassmen with a sand-filled plastic bat. Four football players from the high school were involved, which resulted in suspensions. Principal Jody McCloud is set to resign at the end of the 2004-2005 school year, though uninvolved in the incident.

Central Cabarrus High School
Concord, NC
Baseball team hazing (sexual)
May 4, 2004

Three upperclassmen students, also members of the high school baseball team, reportedly sexually hazed another student in a school locker room. The three students were suspended.

Piedmont Hills High School
San Jose, CA

Football team hazing
September 2004

Varsity football players on the high school team have
reportedly hazed younger players of the junior varsity football
team. The players reportedly pushed a junior varsity team
member. The players were suspended from playing in the
season opener while the investigation continued.

Griffith Senior High School
Griffith, Indiana
Possible soccer hazing incident
September 2004

Older members of the Griffith High School soccer team
reportedly taped other younger members of the team together
and to trees.

Sandwich High School
East Sandwich, MA
Football team hazing
September 14, 2004

Nine Sandwish High School football team members severely
beat a freshman team member. Garrett Watterson was beaten
on the field by varsity players. Watterson was taken to the
emergency room with a ruptured spleen and was hospitalized
after surgery. The nine team members have been charged with
misdemeanors and felonies.

Taunton High School
Taunton, MA
Football team hazing
September 2004

Several members of the Taunton High School football team were suspended after urinating and defecating on freshmen team members' uniforms and equipment, according to The Enterprise.

St. Paul's School
Concord, NH
Sexual natured hazing
September 2004

Twelve freshmen students were hazed by upperclassmen females. The incident involved the senior girls waking up the freshmen student and having them perform and answer sexual natured acts and questions, according to The Concord Monitor. 15 students were suspended.

September 24, 2004

Saint Pius X High School
Pottstown, Pennsylvania
Improper touching during football hazing
2004

In the end no charges were placed against players for alleged sexual hazing, but the head football coach was dismissed and police were reviewing possible charges to levy following an alleged hazing at halftime of a football game.

Milton Area High School
Milton, PA
Football team hazing
October 7, 2004

A football team member paddled a 10th grade team member in a locker room shower. The paddles were made in shop class by the 10th graders, which were then used by the senior football team members.

St. Pius X High School
Pottstown, PA
Suspected sexual natured hazing
August, 2004

Seven members of the high school's football team were suspended for hazing sophomore team members. IcyHot was reportedly put in the sophomore team members' jockstraps.

Glenbrook South High School
Glenview, IL
Lacrosse team hazing
March 12, 2004

13 new team members of the Glenbrook South High School lacrosse team were beaten with a paddle by older team members. Alcohol was involved.

Melvindale High School
Wayne County Michigan
Allegations of sexual assault during hazing
2005 lawsuit

A lawsuit regarding attacks allegedly occurring in 2003 was filed by a former athlete who played for the football team in U.S. District Court in Detroit. The suit criticizes coaches and school officials for their handling of the incident. The suit charges the athlete was held down and molested.

St. Paul's School
Concord, New Hampshire
Allegations of sexual hazing not verified
2004

After some students identified as victims in a sexual simulation case failed to come forward, police concluded they had no case against older students who had allegedly required younger students to simulate sex acts. School officials did discipline seniors, however.

Barnegat High School
Barnegat, New Jersey
Alleged JV football team hazing
September 24, 2004

Hazing allegations involving molestation of a 14-year-old were reported after a party at a residence where a football team member was reportedly held down by other team members and sexually assaulted with a pool stick, according to the ABC-TV web site. Some team members used cell phones to photograph the alleged initiation, according to the Badjocks.com site. Police charged one juvenile with aggravated criminal sexual contact, criminal restraint, assault, and possession of a weapon for an unlawful purpose. Two others were charged with lesser offenses, including the attempted destruction of cell phone evidence.

Colonia High School
Middlesex County, New Jersey
Sexual hazing on soccer team
November 2004

Four soccer players entered guilty please to allegations they put a banana between a player's bare buttocks to simulate a sex act, a common prank at the school according to testimony reported in the Star-Ledger. In the course of the so-called prank, the victim's buttocks had been touched. The players argued they considered the event to be a joke, not an assault. One of those accused of criminal restraint, age 18. went on to play college soccer at a New Jersey College and was interviewed subsequently in an article on campus behavior to say that hazing was not allowed at his new school. Colina High forfeited a game during the investigation. Lawyers for the accused stressed the event was supposed to be a prank, not a hazing, in the minds of their clients.

Western Branch High School
Chesapeake, Virginia
Hazing in which new students were covered in human waste
2004

Two students were offered probation in a hazing case. A letter writer challenges accuracy of newspaper accounts related to the case (May 20, 2008).

Port Hope High School
Port Hope, Michigan
Basketball sexual hazing alleged
2005

After Derek Kessel, a student with learning disabilities, died in a single car crash, police and his parents began pursuing Derek's allegations that he had been taunted and poked inside his buttocks during a hazing meant to humiliate him. Huron County Prosecutor Mark Gaertner told reporters and family there was insufficient evidence of anything other than horseplay and declined to press charges. The alleged hazing case remains disputed by the family. The crash was due to Kessel driving in an unsafe manner, ruled Gaertner. For documents in a lawsuit filed by family and a slideshow, see http://www.mlive.com/flintjournal/porthope/

West High School
Anchorage, Alaska
First-year student paddling
2005

The Anchorage Daily News reported the suspensions of nine upperclassmen in a paddling incident reminiscent of the chasing down of new students in the movie "Dazed and Confused." The school investigation found a number of incidents that occurred in various locales. The paper reported no arrests.

A.H.S.T. (Avoca, Hancock, Shelby, and Tennant Community) High School
Avoca, Iowa
Improper touching with genitals during hazing incident
2005

The adult son of the wrestling coach and four veteran wrestlers received probation on charges they assaulted a younger wrestler and touched or attempted to touch him with their genitals, according to the Council Bluffs Daily Nonpareil.
Ross Pattee, 18, son of coach Gary Pattee who was volunteering his time, acknowledged the hazing and was given probation, according to the paper. Charges against two other accused wrestlers were dropped by the Pottawattamie County District Court because the victim refused to testify against anyone else, according to the Omaha World-Herald.

Plattsmouth High School
Plattsmouth, Nebraska
Improper touching admitted by hazer after sodomy charged by victim
2005

After several varsity players changed their story, a veteran player was cleared of charges he sodomized a player.

The criminal charges against Jacob Schippert for sexual assalt during hazing were not sustained. Schippert was expelled and admitted simulating sex but said the act was meant as a prank and had been done by him to other players on other occasions, according to the World-Herald. The victim claimed he had been anally violated with Schippert's fingers.

Donna High School
Donna, Texas
Sexual assaults claimed during football hazing
2005

In the aftermath of charges that three football players tried to insert fingers into a new player's rectum, the school board fired several coaches and its athletic director. Hidalgo County offered at least three athletes, ages 17 and 19, a diversionary program as an alternative to putting them through a criminal trial.

Fairfield Warde High School
Fairfield, Connecticut
Bondage and poking a hogtied but clothed victim
2005

The "hogtying" ritual described for the first time at a Trumbull, Connecticut school was also practiced here, albeit with a clothed victim. A lacrosse player was prodded and videotaped as he was hazed, according to the Post (Connecticut).

Vestavia Hills High School
Vestavia Hills, Alabama
Breast slamming as initiation claimed by student
2005

An alleged breast slamming initiation was handled quietly by juvenile authorities after a 15-year-old female softball player charged that she was pummeled during an initiation at a motel where the team stayed. A school representative said it appeared nothing more severe than students "playing around" had occurred.

Archbishop Williams High School
Quincy, Massachusetts
Urination on player as hazing
2005 (lawsuit filed)

After an Archbishop Williams hockey star admitted he urinated on a younger player and no charges were filed, the father of the victim sued the school, according to the Patriot Ledger. The player was suspended for one week.

Chapel Rock Youth Camp
Yavapai County, Arizona
Penetration with canes and broomsticks into the clothed bottoms of 18 boys
Summer 2005

While angered parents called for aggravated sexual assault charges to be placed against two counselors for the sexual hazings of at least 18 young campers, a district attorney allowed them to plead guilty to a single lesser count each that resulted in 30 and 45 day sentences apiece. The prosecution accepted the argument that the sexual touching was intended as horseplay and hazing, not rape.

Deer Park High School
Suffolk County, New York
Improper touching during a JV basketball team hazing
January 16, 2006

Two JV players restrained a victim, 13, while another JV basketball player groped the eight-grader in a school locker room. Deer Park High School administrators ended the team's season. The person doing the touching was charged with juvenile delinquency, a lesser offense because he was a juvenile. The basketball coach lost his teaching position.

236

Sierra Vista High School
Las Vegas, Nevada
Conviction on reduced verdict of lewd conduct and battery
February 3, 2006

A basketball player was found not guilty on accusations that he put an object into a 15-year-old player's buttocks, but he was convicted on the lesser charge of touching him on a gym floor during a piling-on by other players.

Wasatch High School
Heber, Utah
Baseball hazing
March 2006

Students were suspended on an away trip after veterans piled on younger players in a motel with resultant groping. The school suspended some participants.

Weber High School
Pleasant View, Utah
Coerced streaking of Warriorettes alleged
April 2006

New female members of the school's drill team claimed they were asked by older members to streak naked across a darkened football field, according to the Deseret Morning News.

Dixon High School
Dixon, California
Paddling during hazing
June 1, 2006

Four males were accused of hitting younger males hard on the buttocks in an initiation held at a female student's house, according to the Sacramento Bee. Police charged the four with hazing. Before the hazing law was tightened in California, a similar incident involving females occurred at the same school.

Fairhaven High School
Fairhaven, Massachusetts
Semen allegedly poured on player during hazing
July 2006

The New Bedford Standard-Times reported that a football player alleged that he had been taped to a bed while bodily fluids were dumped on him during an away football camp. The players were kicked of the team and now face felony charges to answer to the victim's allegations, according to the Boston Globe and Standard-Times.

Spring Grove Area Senior High School
York, Pennsylvania
Improper touching and sexual simulation
August 2006

Seven football players were charged with harassment following a sexually tinged hazing in which players nonetheless had their clothing on. The incident occurred at an away football camp at Albright College in Reading, PA.

Gustine High School
Gustine, California
Allegations of sexual assault
Summer 2006

As of 2007, two veteran players may face criminal charges in an alleged sexual hazing involving football rookies. Two others have also gone through juvenile court for their roles in the incident. The Modesto Bee reported that the assault involved an air pump and used condom. The victim has filed a $3 million claim with the school district. The coach's contract was not renewed.

University of Wisconsin
Madison, Wisconsin
Band hazing with sexual hazing alleged
2006

Long-time UW band director Michael Leckrone found himself on the hot seat after six or more individuals were accused of going over the line with hazing requests, according to the UW student newspaper. The paper editorially defended the director and blamed the individual students for the misbehavior.

Lehi High School
Lehi, Utah
False sexual hazing charged by player
October 2006

A 15-year-old who said he had been victimized in a sexual hazing by football teammates admitted he had made up the tale and was charged as a juvenile for supplying false information to law enforcement. The allegations prior to the admission had created a furor in the community.

San Ramon Valley High School
San Ramon Valley school district, California
Allegations player was kicked in groin
October 2006

The school suspended four JV football players after complaints surfaced that a player was kicked in the groin, given a wedgie, and hazed. The incident was under investigation.

Arlington Country Day School
Jacksonville, Florida

Student athlete taped and made to disrobe in a hazing as punishment
October 29, 2006

School officials fired a coach who punished a 13-year-old player by making him strip to his shorts and run laps. Some players also taped the player with duct tape. The player apparently had ignored the coach's instructions.

Dublin Coffman High School
Dublin, Ohio
Rape allegations against two coaches during hazing
March 2006

Two lacrosse coaches are facing serious charges of aggravated rape and assault which, upon conviction, could result in a 60+ year sentence, according to the Columbus Dispatch. The coaches have been fired, and they and the school district are facing a civil suit filed by a former lacrosse player who says one coach held him down while another coach inserted a gloved finger in him during an away bus trip. The Dispatch quoted the suit as saying the two coaches resurrected a hazing tradition that had been done to them in the 1990s as lacross players at Dublin Scioto High School.

Lexington High School
Lexington, South Carolina
Toilet hazing
March 2006

A freshman baseball player charged that he was injured as five players swarmed him and swirled his head in a toilet. The five were suspended for one week. Two JV coaches who had knowledge of the incident were suspended for the season from coaching (not from teaching), according to The State of Columbia, SC.

Dom Savio High School
Boston, Massachusetts
Coach hazing and sexual assaults
December 2006

Former wrestling coach Everett Bower, 34, pleaded guilty to hazing, raping and sexually assaulting two then-15-year-old wrestlers he had invited to join his handpicked group he called the Disciples, according to the Boston Globe.

Camp Condor
Kern County, California
Allegations of sexual battery and simulation
2006

A mother accused two teen-age counselors of hazing and humiliating her 10-year-old son. Sexual battery charges were filed against one of the teens, according to television station KGET 17. The mother said the teens, though clothes, simulated oral sex with her son.

Molalla High School
Molalla, Oregon
Alleged sexual hazing and one count of alleged sodomy
December 2006

At least five teenage basketball players (oldest age 18) and possibly more will end up in court on felony charges that they sexually hazed a younger player. One is accused of using a finger to penetrate the victim, according to the Oregonian. The hazing attacks were alleged to have occurred in a motel and tea bus during a road trip. The trio are to appear in court in July of 2007.

Whitman-Hanson Regional High School
Whitman, Massachusetts

Athlete allegedly sucker punched in groin
January 2007

Five upperclassmen were suspended when a hazing prank involved hitting a first-year student in the groin while he was taped to a bench, according to the Boston Globe. The school informed police of the incident.

Priest River Lamanna High School
Priest River, Idaho
Alleged sexual hazing by band members
April 2007

Several band members have been charged with a crime on charges they sexually touched a 14-year-old band member with their genitals or placed them near his face as he slept. The band was on a road trip to British Columbia. Three of the accused are 18 years old. Police are studying a videotape made to humiliate the victim.

Flower Mound High School
Denton County, Texas
Hazing admissions and denials
2005-2007

About the only thing residents of Denton County agree upon is that they disagree upon whether antics by veteran wrestlers against new wrestlers at a 2005 pool party at a private residence constituted hazing. A judge ruled that he saw no evidence that compelled him to proceed with hazing charges against a coach and several wrestlers. However, the Dallas Morning News said allegations originally were that the incident was an initiation in which sexual assaults and beatings took place. The Morning News reported that "three juveniles, including at least one initially charged with sexual assault, pleaded true to assault charges in adjudicated agreements." An 18-year-old was given probation, a fine, and community service after pleading no contest to a charge of no contest to a charge of assault with bodily injury, according to the paper.

South Hills High School
Fort Worth, Texas
Alleged "swirlie" on younger teammate
March 2007

Eight baseball players were suspended for an undisclosed locker room attack on a fellow student. The Fort Worth Star-Telegram quoted a mother who said the incident was the dunking of a younger player's head into a toilet. The paper said the school decided it would not seek criminal charges against any of the eight.

Glenbard East High School
Lombard, Illinois
Urinating on a teammate called a prank, not criminal hazing
2007

School officials have maintained that the locker room attack of a baseball player urinating on a younger teammate as three mates held the boy down was a prank, not hazing, recalling similar school denials made in many other instances. According to the Daily Herald, a local police chef ruled it was a matter for school officials to punish, not a criminal matter. Those making the ruling that they considered the event non-hazing were Bob McBride, the school's principal, the coach Nick Scipione, and Police Chief Raymond Byrne. Not even a police report was filed, according to the Daily Herald.

Austin High School
Austin, Minnesota
Allegations of intent to improperly touch during a hazing
(2007)

A teenager charged he was able to fend off two nude older hockey teammates attempting to grope him in a meeting room adjoining the school's locker room. One faces a criminal trial. Most serious is the charge one is facing which is a felony charge of aiding and abetting indecent exposure, according to the Post-Bulletin of Rochester, MN. The two were suspended for three days.

Coopersville High School
Coopersville, Michigan
Investigation into alleged penetration with object and groping
June 2007

Four JV players were under suspension as law enforcement authorities from the Ottawa County Sheriff's Department conducted interviews into allegations that a 15-year-old was abused in a group hazing, according to The Press of Grand Rapids, MI. No charges had been placed as of this writing. The alleged incident was to have taken place in a locker room. Four students served 10-day suspensions. The JV coach resigned and told The Press some of the hazing might have begun in April of 2007.

International Allegations of Sexual Hazing

Nakhimov Naval School
Leningrad, Russia
Allegations of beating and sexual abuse of cadets
February 2003

Three cadets aged 14 and under and their parents accused upperclassmen of multiple beatings and one sexual assault during hazing incidents.

Warren Elementary School
Canada
Injuries during paddling
April 17, 2003

Several members of Warren Collegiate were suspended after five seventh and eighth grade boys sustained severe injuries to their buttocks after being paddled with a cricket bat. The school is located about 20 miles north of Winnipeg.

McGill University
Montreal, Canada
Sexual hazing alleged in football initiation
2005

Charges and denials flew when a football player announced that he had been sexually touched by teammates in an initiation. Part of the season was cancelled by authorities. The controversy flamed when a small-paper journalist named the victim and his father, a well-known Canadian journalist. University officials found evidence of nudity and use of a broomstick in hazing rituals.

Simon Fraser University
Vancouver, Canada
Sexual simulation during hazing
2006

At least seven swimming and diving team members were asked to simulate sex in a photographed hazing ritual at a private residence. Administrators banned the team from National Association of Intercollegiate Athletics championship competition as a punishment